DEVON AND CORNWALL RECORD SOCIETY

New Series, Vol. 32

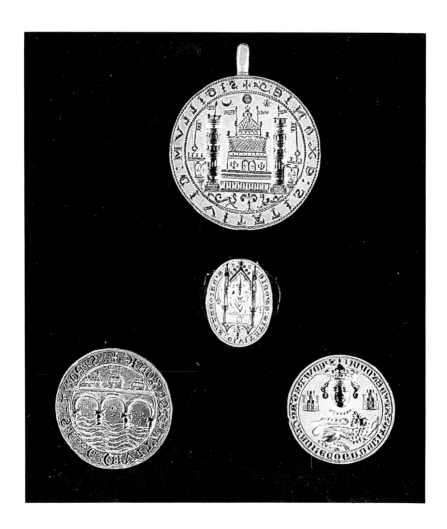

MATRICES OF EXETER SEALS
(preserved in the Exeter City Archives)

(*top*)   Exeter city seal, *circa* 1200, made by one Luke and paid for by a wealthy citizen, William Prudum. Legend: +SIGILLVM CIVITATIS EXONIE. Silver.

(*centre*)   Exeter mayoralty seal, 13th cent. Legend: S' MAIORATVS: CIVITATIS: EXONIE. Silver.

(*bottom left*)   Exe Bridge seal, *circa* 1250. Legend: +S' PONTIS:EXE: CIVITATIS: EXONIE. Lead.

(*bottom right*)   Seal of the statute merchant (the king's seal), late 13th cent., granted by Edward I to the mayor for the recognizances of debts. Legend: S' EDW' REG' ANGL' AD RECOGN' DEBITOR' APVD EXONIA. Silver.

DEVON & CORNWALL RECORD SOCIETY

New Series, Vol. 32

THE RECEIVERS' ACCOUNTS

OF THE CITY OF EXETER

1304–1353

Edited and translated with an Introduction by

MARGERY M. ROWE and JOHN M. DRAISEY

1989

ISBN 0 901853 32 1

Printed for the Society by
BPCC Wheatons Ltd.,
Hennock Road, Exeter, England

CONTENTS

and the next surviving one of 1339–1340, the headings are similar. All the accounts translated here place the Charge (receipts) first; this is followed by the Discharge (expenditure) although there are some variations in the order of the sub-sections within the two and, finally, there is a statement of what remains over or owing if applicable and, if given, the names of the auditors.

There are some inconsistencies regarding the dating of the first extant receiver's roll. The heading describes it as the account of Robert de Nyweton', seneschal[1] (*not* receiver) in the 34th year of Edward I. It has been assumed hitherto that the account related to the year Michaelmas 33—Michaelmas 34 Edward I, i.e. 29 September 1305 to 29 September 1306. However, there are two accounts on this roll: the income and expenditure sections for the year described as 34 Edward I and on the dorse of the roll, the income section only for a year described as an account of 'Robert de Neweton, seneschal for the year xxx . . . [to] Edward I'. It is assumed that this is the account for the year following but if so, it should have been described as 1 Edward II, i.e. the account for the year Michaelmas 1306 to Michaelmas 1307. It is therefore likely that the years represented in this roll are 1304–1305 and 1305–1306 and this is confirmed by the totals given for admissions to the freedom of the city.[2] Robert de Nyweton' was seneschal in both of these years[3] and it is reasonable that he should account for both. The only possible argument against the 1304–1306 dating is that the first account includes payments to Philip Deneband and his clerk. In the year 1304–1305 Philip Deneband[4] is described as *clericus* and in the following year as *ballivus* but is is quite possible that even as *clericus* he employed a sub-clerk.

The rolls translated here are on parchment and written in Latin. Apart from the roll for 1304–1306 which is torn, stained and creased, most are in good condition. The roll for 1347–1348 is faded and there is a large hole in the second section of the roll for 1341–1342. The rolls for 1339–1340, 1342–1343, 1349–1350, 1350–1351, 1351–1352 and 1352–1353 have two membranes, bound 'exchequer fashion', i.e. head to tail. The remainder have a single membrane. Where the rolls are written on both sides, a note has been made in the text. It is interesting to note that there is a duplicate roll for the receivership of Robert Brown (1350–1351) which consists of three membranes bound 'chancery fashion', i.e. all joined at the head. It was evidently the accepted practice that the final accounts should follow the pipe roll and other accounts emanating from the central government in the way they were made up.

There seems little difference in the arrangement of the receivers' rolls

[1]*Senescallus* has been translated as seneschal, being nearer to the Latin than bailiff or steward. The city had four seneschals.

[2]The total receipts from entrants in 1304–1305 is given in the mayor's court rolls as £10 6s 8d (*Exeter Freemen*). The total in 1305–1306 is given in the mayor's court rolls as £5 3s 4d plus a voluntary payment, which could well have been 13s 4d, giving the total of £5 16s 8d which coincides with that given in the second income section of the first receiver's roll.

[3]DRO, ECA, MCR 32–33 Ed.I, m.Id. and MCR 33–34 Ed.I, m.4d.

[4]R.C. Easterling, 'List of Civic Officials of Exeter of the 12th and 13th centuries', *TDA* lxx (1938) pp. 455–494, gives the name as Deneband and is in error in giving the fee as £4. Deneband/Denebaud are indistinguishable in contemporary scripts but Deneband has been preferred in modern works.

before and after some 'directions' given by the city's government *circa* 1340 as to the order of making up the receivers' accounts.[1] These stated that the accounts were to include rents of assize, sale of pasture in the city and suburbs, bagavel and brithingavel, custom of fish, custom of meat, custom of cloth and other small customs, issues of the pyx, customs from the toll of ships (town duties), perquisites of courts, issues of murage when murage is granted, fines for entering the freedom of the city, customs of oil, customs of measuring corn and flour, chattels of felons and fugitives, rent of the common well and increment of rents.

THE OFFICE OF RECEIVER

There is no evidence for any receivers in any records before Robert de Nyweton is mentioned in the roll for 1304–6.[2] The mayor's court rolls extant for the period 1307–1338, for which no receivers' rolls exist, list receivers amongst the city's officers elected at Michaelmas for the years 1311–1314, 1318–1325, 1326–1329, 1330–1331 and 1338–1339 and it is very probable that in the years when a receiver was not mentioned as such one of the four seneschals undertook the duty.[3] By 1339–1340 the receiver is described as 'seneschal and receiver of the common goods of the City of Exeter'. There is no medieval account of his duties but a sixteenth-century one given by John Hooker the city's chamberlain and historian has some bearing even on the duties 200 years earlier.[4] Hooker states that the receiver has the charge of three several officers, i.e. the other three stewards or seneschals. He is always one of the Twenty-Four and Common Council (i.e. the ruling councillors of the city) and he is to see true records to be made, true justice to be kept and all records to be safely laid up at the year's end. He may not stay outside the city without the mayor's licence, he must attend the markets, and ensure all victuals to be wholesome, the assizes of bread and ale to be kept and all weights and measures to be just. He is to receive and collect all rents and money due to the city and defray the charges of the same; to seeing that no false records are entered but that the records are kept safe. At his year's end he is to make a true account of all his receipts and payments before the auditors.

In 1339 it appears that the duties were not carried out to this standard of perfection. Nicholas Godiscote, former receiver, refused to make his account and was arrested. He promised to do so by the following Monday 'but contrary to his promyse he went and fledd unto Toppesham where he kept hym self untyll a further order was taken'.[5] The outcome is not recorded but the incident could explain the fact that are no receivers' rolls extant for the period 1306–1307 to 1338–1339 and there is no evidence that

---

[1] DRO, ECA, Miscellaneous Roll 2, no. 35.

[2] Easterling, (above, note 4, p. viii).

[3] Above, note 1, p. viii; Dr. Easterling, (above, note 4, p. viii) lists officers up to 1330–1331 only. J.J. Alexander, 'Leading Civic officials of Exeter 1330–1537', *TDA* lxx (1938), pp. 405–421 continues the list for the period under review.

[4] W.J. Harte, J.W. Schopp and H. Tapley Soper, eds., *The Description of the Citie of Excester by John Vowell alias Hooker*, 3 vols., DCRS (1919 and 1947), pp. 809–810.

[5] ECA, Book 51 (Hooker's Commonplace Book), f.273.

the missing rolls were seen by John Hooker in the sixteenth century. The roll for 1339–1340 begins with the arrears received on the account of Nicholas de Godiscote (53s 4d) so the city recovered these from him.

In 1340, as part of the constitutional crisis in the government of the city,[1] orders were given that the mayor and his *locum tenens* were not to meddle with the administration of the goods of the city, but the receiver only was to deal with these. The orders also stated that the receiver was bound to render account immediately after his year of office had ended.[2] The first order may relate to items which appear in the receivers' accounts as sanctioned by the *probi homines* (presumably referring to the councillors) or to the condoning of amercements by the mayor and seneschals,[3] but similar entries continue to appear after 1340. As to the second order, undoubtedly some time elapsed before the written account could be submitted. The draft copy of the roll of Robert Brown already mentioned was made apparently because the account was of greater complexity than usual; it cannot be assumed that a draft copy was always made. The account for 1348–1349 has a memorandum that the bailiffs' accounts were delivered to John Gyst, the receiver, to transcribe and return within eight days and there is a note that the account was paid on the Tuesday after the feast of St. Barnabas 25 Edward III (14 June 1351) which was two years after John Gyst had completed his year of office. The roll for 23–24 Edward III (1349–1350) has a note that the account of rents was made on the Wednesday in the feast of St. Thomas the Apostle 25 Edward III (21 December 1351), and obviously there were loose ends to be tied up. The rolls would have been written up by a clerk or sub-clerk whose fee of 10s is accounted for in the 'Fees and Pensions' section of the rolls.

There was no *cursus honorum*, or regular progression from the office of receiver to that of mayor, mainly because the latter was often held repeatedly (there were only sixteen different mayors in the fifty years between 1304 and 1354), whereas it was unusual for a man to be receiver more than once. Nevertheless at least ten of the sixteen mayors had previously been receivers, and perhaps more, since before 1304 it is not possible to tell which of the four seneschals, if any, had acted as receiver. The proportion rises to seven out of eight between 1335 and 1354. The exception, Thomas de Lychefeld, was first elected to replace Martin le Keu, who died in office during the year 1334–1335. Receivers frequently appear as seneschals again after their term of office whereas mayors do not.

Hooker records in his annals under the year 1347–1348 that there was a great contention in the city concerning the election of the mayor and officers and that it was ordered from henceforth that none should be chosen nor admitted mayor except he be a 'wyse, grave, sobre and honest man' and had been a steward for one whole year. The mayor was also to have a freehold of £5 per annum.[4] These orders reflect what the city saw as the right qualifications for its mayors and receivers to possess. Unfortunately there are few references in other sources to those who acted as receiver in

[1] *Medieval Council*, p. 33, where there is a fuller discussion.
[2] ECA, Miscellaneous Roll 2.
[3] See the roll for 1304–1306 under the Section 'Amercements condoned and not levied' and the roll for 1339–1340 under 'Allowances of the Serjeants.'
[4] ECA, Book 51, annals, *sub* 1347.

the period under review, apart from their membership of the common council as listed in the mayor's court rolls,[1] with the exception of Robert de Brideport, sometimes called Robert de Beaminster, who acted as the king's agent in several capacities as well as occupying the offices of mayor and member of parliament for the city.[2] John Gyst is described as a collector of customs in 1361.[3] Robert Brown was licensed to ship corn to Gascony in 1352[4] and Thomas le Spicer was involved in a case concerning wine dues in 1342.[5] John de Neweton, mercer, was assessed at 40d in the 1332 lay subsidy and Robert de Bradeworthi at 10s in the same document.[6] John Spicer was appointed a customs collector from Bristol to Exeter in 1349 and acknowledged his indebtedness to William de Exon in 1357.[7] It is interesting to note that the wills of no less than three receivers in the period under review—John Spicer, Robert Brown and Richard Olyver—were proved on the mayor's court roll on the same day, 22 November 1361. Robert Brown and John Spicer had been elected to the Common Council as late as Michaelmas 1360. The deaths may have been caused by the plague which returned to the city in 1360–1361.[8]

A comparison of the names of receivers with admissions to the city freedom reveals that most receivers were freemen. Reginald Wythoun was admitted on 22 May 1329, Robert de Bradeworthy, cordwainer, on 27 September 1322, John de Nyweton on 19 December 1317, Thomas le Spicer on 30 January 1335, John Gist (of Wreyford) on 29 September 1337, John Spycer on either 13 April 1349 or 20 September 1350, Robert Brown on 16 November 1338 at the request of Roger, vicar of Heavitree, and John Swaneton on 22 September 1337. There is no admission for Robert de Brideport but his son claimed the freedom by succession on 15 April 1359, his father's will having been proved on the Mayor's Court roll in 1358. Richard Oliver (spelt differently from the receiver Richard Olyver of Kingston) was admitted on 5 September 1334. No admission can be traced for Robert de Nyweton, receiver in 1304–1306, but it is accepted that there was an under-recording of admissions in the late thirteenth century and Robert de Nyweton may have been fairly elderly when he took office as his will is dated 1311.[9]

---

[1] *Medieval Council*, pp. 69–70; *DCNO* xix (1936–7), p. 170.
[2] *TDA* lix (1927), pp. 298, 305–6; *TDA* lx (1928), p. 213; *TDA* lxx (1938), pp. 410–411, 416; *HMC Calendar of the Manuscripts of the Dean and Chapter of Wells*, II [Cd. 7106], 1914, p. 616 (where he is described as clerk of the king for debtors' recognizances in Exeter); *Cal. FR, 1347–56*, pp. 218 and 253 (apointment to collect the naval subsidy in the port of Exeter in 1350). There also appears to have been a son of the same name which confuses the issue. A will of a Robert de Brideport is proved on the mayor's court roll on 23 July 1358.
[3] *Cal. FR, 1356–68*, p. 156; his will was proved on the mayor's court roll on 18 March 1381. A release of a garden at Taddiford, in St. David's parish, Exeter, on 21 August 1348, has the reference ECA, ED/M/377.
[4] *Cal. PR, 1350–42*, pp. 358–9.
[5] *Cal. CR, 1341–3*, p. 475.
[6] Audrey M. Erskine, *The Devonshire Lay Subsidy of 1332*, DCRS (NS. vol 14). pp. 109–110.
[7] *Cal. FR, 1347–56*, p. 135; *Cal. CR, 1354–60*, pp. 313 and 427.
[8] ECA, Book 51. Hooker notes in his annals for this year that 'the descease of the pestylens beganne throughe the whole realme and wherewth this Citie was miche infected. Also there fell greate stormes off tempestes whereby many churches houses & steples were overthrown'.
[9] *Exeter Freemen* pp. xiii–xiv, 4–30. The wills proved in the mayor's court rolls are listed in a folder in the Devon Record Office's search room.

THE CITY'S INCOME: RENTS RECEIVED

This section in the account rolls includes rents from property in the city (sometimes described as petty rents), rent for the farm of the manor of Duryard, rents received for the passage (ferry) and house at *Prattishide* in Littleham (Exmouth) parish and the cash received from the customs of bagavel and brithgavel.[1] (These terms are explained on p.xiii). It is fortunate that a rental of the city's property survives[2] and this is printed in translation at Appendix II(i) on pages 90–93. Apart from the farm of Duryard, which is written twice in this rental, the rents total just under £9. Three years later the receiver accounted for £8 1s 9d from petty rents. In 1339–1340 the amount is only £6 6s 4d and with the exception of the year 1347–1348 when the sum has dropped to £3 17s 6d, possibly attributable to non-collection because of the Black Death, the sum remains fairly constant. The sums from these rents represented a very modest percentage of the city's income, less than a third of the sum realised by the farm of the manor of Duryard.

Duryard had belonged to the city of Exeter from time immemorial. It stretched from the walls of Exeter northwards to the river at Cowley Bridge and was a Saxon deer-park. In 1276 the manor of Duryard, Cowley and *Goseforde* was leased to Alured de la Porte for ten years at a rental of £10.[3] In 1304–1306 and 1339–1340 the rent was £25 12s 6d. No payment was made for it in 1341–1342 but the rent was raised to £30 in 1342–1343[4] and again to £32 in 1349–1350. The 'Regulations' of the city issued in 1345 provided for rents exceeding £25 12s 6d from the manor of Duryard to be placed in the chest in the custody of the four good men of the city.[5] From 1368 there are separate account rolls for the manor of Duryard.

By an agreement of 1265–1266 the abbot and convent of Sherborne released to the city the passage or ferry over the water of Checkston (i.e. *Prattishide* ferry) provided the monks and all men of their *familia* were able to pass free. They also gave up the right to the toll which the city levied on goods coming into the manor of Littleham.[6] The receiver's account roll for 1304–1306 does not mention the passage but the roll for 1339–1340 includes income of 28s from the passage and a house at *Prattishide* and this sum remains constant until 1347–1348 when the rent drops to 7s 8d. From 1348–1353 the house is included in the petty rents figure, but nothing is received from the passage as the boat is completely broken. According to a lease of 1542 the plot consisted of 'a piece of land next the sea at Exmouth measuring 110 feet x 80 feet'.[7] Exmouth was within the port of Exeter and the city wished to control its collection of town customs throughout the port but the ferry as such seems to have yielded very little in the way of income.

---

[1] In the roll for 1304–1306 bagavel and brithgavel income is placed under 'Issues of the City'.
[2] ECA, Miscellaneous Roll 2, no.28.
[3] ECA, Miscellaneous Roll 2, no.37.
[4] In this year the receiver also accounted for 10s for the purchase of two acres of land of Matilda Oblyn which Hamo de Dirworthi [the king's justice of assize] held in the manor of Duryard. The original 'grant' of these two acres, where no purchase sum is mentioned, survives (ECA, ED/M/350).
[5] ECA, Miscellaneous Roll 2, no.32.
[6] ECA, Miscellaneous Roll 2, no.34.
[7] ECA, ED/M/1047.

THE CITY'S INCOME: ISSUES OF THE CITY

Bagavel and brithgavel appear under both 'Issues of the City' and 'Profits of the Courts'. An exact definition of the words cannot be given but it is likely that they were taxes paid by those who did not possess the freedom of the city for selling ale (brithgavel) and bread (bagavel).[1] The words are spelt in various ways in the receivers' rolls and the sums collected vary from £4 in 1339–1340 to £2 3s in 1342–1343. The roll for 1304–1306 includes 9s 6d for half of the brithgavel in St. Sidwell's presumably because the dues were shared between the city and the owners of St. Sidwell's fee, the dean and chapter of Exeter. No payments for bagavel and brithgavel appear on the receivers' rolls for 1348–1353. These particular customs were still being farmed out by the city in the sixteenth century.[2]

Under the heading of 'Issues of the City', the receiver accounted for all customs collected from those who were not freemen of the city but who sold goods there,[3] from those who took fur out of the city which attracted a special duty,[4] and from sums paid as town custom, petty custom or town duty levied in the port of the city of Exeter. These latter duties were granted by a charter of Edward III but separate customs rolls exist from the reign of Edward I which give a detailed breakdown of the payments by individual ships on certain products coming into the port, mostly landed at Topsham. Duties on wine are shown separately as the city was entitled to only two thirds of the sums collected, the rest being payable to the earl of Devon as for his manor of Topsham. The one third paid to the earl is shown under 'Rents paid' in the receivers' rolls. As already mentioned, these customs will be discussed more fully by Dr Kowaleski in her edition of the customs rolls. The receivers' rolls show variations in the sums collected from £7 18s 3d to £23 3s 4½d, the former total covering the year 1348–49 and presumably because of the Black Death. These totals would seem to give a better indication of the state of the city's economy than some of the other sections' totals of receipts.

'Issues of the pyx' are listed under 'Issues of the City' and 'Profits of the Courts' in these rolls. The pyx was presumably the chest in the custody of the four good men of the city referred to in the 'Regulations' of 1345 for the excess of rents of the manor of Duryard (*supra*, p. xii) but there may have been more than one chest. At the end of the receiver's roll for 1349–1350 is a note that 10s 5½d is in the custody of the mayor in the chest in the provostry with the cash of the lord king's collection[5] and a memorandum at the end of the roll for 1350–1351 states that 6s is in the keeping of the mayor

[1]For a discussion of these terms see George Oliver, *op.cit.*, p. 310; for 'particulars of such duties as do the appertaine to Bagavell' see ECA, Book 52, f.244 and for details of the farm of bagavel and brithgavel see ECA, Book 57, f.1. Customs receipts, including bagavel and brithgavel, are occasionally entered on the mayor's court rolls.

[2]ECA, ED/M/1053; ED/M/1100.

[3]J.W. Schopp (ed.), *The Anglo-Norman Custumal of Exeter*, Exeter, 1925, introduction.

[4]Skinners were permitted to sell furs in the city without custom because of watch and ward of the city which they provided. If the furs were removed from the city, custom had to be paid (MCR 17–18 Ed.I, m.19d).

[5]H. Lloyd Parry, *Exeter Guildhall*, Exeter, 1936, p. 8, has a reference for 1390–1 to a legal document which was entered at the Assizes being placed in a certain chest in the provostry called the Boffet.

with the other cash. In the roll for the following year, cash or quittances are noted as being placed in the pyx. It presumably represented the city's "contingency fund" but was on a rather small scale. Finally, there was also some income from letting out grazing but this varied considerably.

THE CITY'S INCOME: PROFITS OF THE COURTS

These 'profits' derived from several sources: fines collected in the mayor's court, presumably fines of the provost's court[1] (although these are never distinguished as such), fines of the mayor's tourn[2] (these usually appear on a separate line in the receivers' rolls), fines for false measures (so described in 1341–1342 and 1351–1352 and the same as the amercements of the examination of the measures itemised in 1349–1350), the amercements of the bakers (for short weight and poor quality), estreats for St. Nicholas' fair and the goods of felons and waifs and strays. A note of the goods of felons is sometimes entered on the mayor's court rolls.[3] The city had claimed the profits of its courts from time immemorial. A royal charter of exemplification of 1365 granted at the instance of the mayor, bailiffs and commonalty of the city confirmed to them the return of writs, estreats, fines, pleas of unjustly taking away cattle, gallows, pillory, tumbrel, amends of assize of ale, waif, forefeng, a coroner of their own; also a fair at the gule of August for four days and a market for three days in the week, as they had had from the time of the Conquest.[4]

A fragment of a table of rates of customs levied in the fair, dating from the time of Henry III, survives on a roll in the City Archives and the same source has a note possibly added in the late fourteenth century that whereas the late serjeants of the court of the city have been negligent in levying the amercements of the extracts of the said court and the receivers have not audited their accounts of the same, it is agreed that the receiver shall take account of the said amercements at the end of every quarter.[5] It was probably much the same fifty years earlier, as the collection of the profits of the courts must have represented one of the most complex parts of the accounting operation. This is shown in particular by the receiver's roll for 1350–1351, when many amercements were condoned by the mayor and other officers. In some cases the amercements are described as 'wrong' and in other cases they were not able to be levied. The reasons for these are not given but probably occurred because four serjeants were dealing with

---

[1]Although there was an Exeter official called the provost, the provost's court rolls appear to be the adjourned sessions of the mayor's court when presumably the mayor was not present. The records of the provost's court are enrolled separately from 1328, previous entries having been made on the mayor's court rolls. Fines are totalled on the provost's court rolls at the end of each membrane.

[2]The mayor's tourn rolls are extant from 1337–1338. They record presentments made by the juries in each quarter of the city of nuisances, selling by bad measure and similar offences. Before 1337 the proceedings appear to have been recorded on the mayor's court rolls.

[3]MCR 26–27 Edward III, extracts from which are printed in George Oliver, *op.cit.*, pp. 312–319, has a note of a mazer bowl, mounted with silver, waived by a thief. This appears in RR for 1352–1353 as 'one cup taken from the hands of a thief'.

[4]ECA, Charter XXI.

[5]ECA, Miscellaneous Roll 2.

amercements imposed in at least three separate courts for a wide variety of offences. Evidently the serjeants collected goods as well as cash in payment of fines, as a list of articles taken by John Stam as amercements survives for 1333–1334.[1]

An unusual entry under 'Profits of Courts' appears in the receiver's roll for 1348–1349. Robert de Lucy, bailiff, was paid 16s in fees for wills proved for five weeks during the Black Death's visitation. Totals for the amounts received annually for fines from entries by purchase to the freedom of the city appear on all the receivers' rolls in this volume. An examination of the freemen's list shows that the payments by individuals varied widely for the period 1304–1353.[2] In theory the totals should agree with those given in the receivers' rolls, where they exist, but there are discrepancies for some years.[3] The totals from the two sources are as follows:

	Mayor's Court rolls			*Receivers' rolls*		
1304–1305	£10	6s	8d	£10	6s	8d
1305–1306	£5	3s	4d and a	£5	16s	8d
	voluntary payment					
1339–1340	£9	16s	0d	£10	2s	8d
1341–1342	£10	5s	8d	£9	. . . (entry defective)	
1342–1343	£11	2s	0d	£9	12s	8d
1344–1345	£7	5s	4d	£7	5s	4d
1347–1348	£8	16s	8d	£7	18s	8d
1348–1949	£15	2s	8d	£15	0s	0d
1349–1350	£8	0s	8d	£8	0s	8d
1350–1351	£3	2s	8d	£1	13s	4d
1351–1352	£1	19s	4d	£1	19s	4d
1352–1353	£3	0s	0d	£3	0s	0d

There was also a considerable variation in the sums raised each year but in general (the Black Death year of 1348–9 is a possible exception), the admissions do not appear to have been used as an income raiser; rather the city was more concerned with the necessity to restrict the freedom and its privileges so that it could maintain control over trade.

THE CITY'S EXPENDITURE

As with the income portion of the rolls, the expenditure section is divided under headings which seem to have been already fixed in 1304–1306 although the headings are not necessarily in the same order in every roll.[4] Towards the end of the period under review, additional headings were created to take care of certain projects such as the expenses on building

---

[1]ECA, ED/M/314.

[2]*Exeter Freemen*, pp. 8–30

[3]The situation seems to have been similar later in the fourteenth century. See M.E. Curtis, 'Admission to Citizenship in Fourteenth Century Exeter', *TDA* lxiii (1931), pp. 265–272.

[4]For page references to the headings of income and expenditure see page xxiv.

work on the city walls in 1351–1352 and expenses on the chapel above the East Gate in 1352–1353. There is also some slight variation in what entries appear under which section.

THE CITY'S EXPENDITURE: RENTS PAID

Three entries appear constantly under this heading in the rolls: a payment for the fee farm of the city (which was a fixed rent payable in composition of any dues which the overlord had the right to collect), a payment to the prior of Holy Trinity London and a rent or donation to the parish chaplains or rectors of Exeter. The receiver also accounts for sums paid to the earl of Devon for one third of the wine landed at Topsham as stated in the section on 'Issues of the city'.

The citizens of Exeter received a grant of the fee farm from Richard king of the Romans by virtue of his rights as earl of Cornwall in 1259. The earldom, with the city and castle of Exeter as an appendage, had been granted to him by his brother, King Henry III. The grant was considered a privilege and it was confirmed to the city by Henry III who specified that the fee farm rent was to be £13 9s annually.[1] In the fourteenth century the arrangement was questioned by the Crown and quashed by the Exchequer after litigation lasting from 1324–1332.[2] In 1332 a charter of Edward III specified that the fee farm rent was to be £20 'because it was found that the city was of the ancient demesne of the Crown and that the king had no estate in the city but only the farm of £12 19s'.[3] The latter sum is presumably an error for £13 9s in the 1259 grant. The £20 fee farm rent was ordered to be paid to Edward duke of Cornwall (the Black Prince) by a writ to the mayor of Exeter on 24 July 1337 and payments began on 28 September 1337.[4] Payments of this £20 for the fee farm are standard in the receivers' rolls for 1339–1353, apart from £19 paid in 1341–1342, possibly a clerical error. In the roll for 1304–1305, it is noted that nothing was paid 'to the earl marshal' for the farm of the city and the annual payment may have lapsed before the litigation in the Exchequer referred to above.

In addition to the payment of the fee farm, the city paid an annual rent to the priory of Holy Trinity, Aldgate, London and this payment dated from the reign of Henry I.[5] The standard payment in the receivers' rolls in the first half of the fourteenth century was £25 12s 6d per annum.[6] In 1351–1352 the receiver accounted for the payment for one term only; no

[1] ECA, Charters XI and XII.

[2] *Medieval Council*, p. xiv.

[3] ECA, Charter XX.

[4] *Cal. CR, 1337–9*, p. 198.

[5] The original charter for this grant does not survive but there is a transcript at ECA, Transcripts 2001. In 1482 the prior of Holy Trinity acknowledged the receipt of £12 16s 3d paid to him by the mayor of Exeter, due to the priory by the alms of the king's progenitors (ECA, ED/M/889).

[6] This was, in fact, the same sum yielded to the city for the rent of Duryard in 1304–1306 and 1339–1340 and is the amount specified for Duryard in the rental (see Appendix II, i). In the latter document 'empty because it belongs to the City of London' is written by the side of the entry, which may indicate that the rent was not real income but that it was used as a 'trade-off' for the rent paid to Holy Trinity, London.

payment was made in 1341–1342 and in 1339–1340 no less than £71 5s 0d was paid but the sum included the arrears of previous years. An item under 'Necessary Expenses' in the roll for 1348–1349 for a payment to William Hynelonde, attorney of John Cory, for John's work to discharge the city from the sum of £67 which was exacted annually by the earl of Devon in the pipe (roll) for the farm of the city in arrears may refer to this, although it is eight years later. Otherwise the meaning of this entry is unclear. A petition of 1422 mentions the fee farm rent of £45.12s 6d[1] which unlike some of the references in the city charters, agrees with the sum recorded in the receiver's rolls as what the city was paying.

The regular payment of 4s 8d to the parish chaplains, or rectors, appears to represent the sum of 2d yearly paid by the 'Provostry' (presumably meaning the city's officer called the provost) to twenty-eight chapels in the city, mentioned in the Custumal of Exeter which was drawn up not later than 1242. The Custumal states that each chapel where there is a parish is entitled to receive from this source one penny on St. Martin's Day (in November) and another on Hockday (the second Tuesday after Easter).[2]

The amounts listed under 'Rent Deficits' and 'Rents Allowed' in the receivers' rolls are normally small sums, often for gates and steps and for property which has been allowed to fall into disrepair or because it is empty. Many of the same entries appear year after year, presumably because there had been no attempt to update the rental of 1302–1303, where the property was listed. Several of the properties adjoin the city's gates and walls and the city would have held these properties from an early date for defence purposes. The site of *Hangemannesplace*, noted as being outside the East Gate, is of interest in revealing either a local place of execution or just simply the hangman's house. The allowances to the serjeants for amercements levied in the courts appear in the 'Rents Allowed' section in 1348–1349, apparently in error, and this accounts for the total sum of over £10, a much larger sum than usual in the section in this year.

THE CITY'S EXPENDITURE: NECESSARY EXPENSES

Under this heading in the accounts appear the sums spent on the city's buildings with payments to the workmen employed on repairs, both as wages and food and drink. Occasionally the sustenance provided for the city's officers is also listed here but is just as likely to appear under 'Expenses and Payments', 'Gifts and Presents' or 'Fees paid'.

The city must have assumed ownership of its Guildhall and of the city gates at an early date and would have counted itself responsible for their maintenance well before the date of the first extant receiver's roll of 1304–1306. The Guildhall was on its present site at least as early as 1289 when John de Butelesgate undertook to pay to the mayor one penny each year for the easement of attaching a beam of his house to the hall. This payment was raised to 2d in the reign of Charles II and up to 1974 the owners of the building next to the Guildhall, 'The Turks Head', still paid

---

[1] ECA, Miscellaneous Roll 3, item XVII.
[2] J.W. Schopp (ed.), *Anglo-Norman Custumal of Exeter*, p. 33.

an identical sum to Exeter City Council. John Hooker, writing in the sixteenth century stated in his annals under the year 1330 that 'This yere the Guyldhall of the Citie of Exeter was buylded' but no other evidence now remains as to the extent of this work and it may not necessarily mean a complete new building.[1] If the building depicted on the first common seal of the city (see frontispiece) represented the Guildhall in the late twelfth century, it seems that major changes were made to the building as it would be difficult to reconcile this with the present building, even without its Elizabethan portico, but the seal evidence cannot be relied on. In 1339–1340, nine years later than the supposed rebuilding, the receiver's roll contains a reference to 12s 8d spent on the Guildhall pentice and to locks made for the Guildhall cellar. Sums spent on the window, the roof and the Guildhall garden were accounted for in the 1342–1343 roll and more work on the Guildhall roof in 1344–1345, 1348–1349, 1350–1351, 1351–1352 and 1352–1353, which looks as if either an annual sum was set aside for this purpose or that the roof was particularly troublesome. The frequency of the maintenance in these years seems to argue against a complete rebuilding of the Guildhall in 1330, however.

The city had been empowered to raise a toll of murage for the building and maintenance of its walls since the reign of Henry III. Only small sums from this source appear in the receivers' rolls in the period 1304–1353, the highest amounts being in 1350–51 when over £1 was spent on a bridge at the East Gate and in the following year when £1 12s 6d was expended. This was because the main expenditure was accounted for in separate murage rolls. The murage roll for 1341–1342, which appears to be written in the same hand as the receiver's roll, is printed as Appendix II, ii, in this volume (see pp. 93–110). In that account more than £23 was expended during the forty weeks specified and this amount is more consistent with the £10 which the Crown ordered the sheriff of Devon to spend on the repair of houses, towers, gates and buildings of Exeter Castle in June 1339.[2] The Crown and not the city had the responsibility of maintaining the castle.

Neither the murage roll for 1341–1342 nor the receiver's roll of the same year refer to work which the city was ordered to undertake in February 1340 on blocking up and narrowing the cemetery gates round the Cathedral Close.[3] This was necessary because several men of the city had made walls, houses and buildings contiguous to the Cathedral cemetery, containing gates, posterns and windows so wide that men and women entered the cemetery at night. This work may have been done almost immediately, in the year 1340–1341, for which no receiver's roll and murage roll survive. The cathedral fabric accounts for 1340–1341 include sums spent on repairing the gate of the Close near the archdeacon of Exeter's house.[4] Heavier expenditure on the city walls is recorded in the period after 1350.[5] No expenses for the repair of Exe Bridge appear in the

[1] For a fuller discussion of the early history of the Guildhall see H. Lloyd-Parry *The History of the Exeter Guildhall and the Life within*, Exeter, 1936, pp. 1–20. Lloyd Parry used the receiver's roll to ascertain the nature and extent of repairs made to the building.

[2] *Cal. CR, 1339–41*, p. 166.

[3] *Ibid.*, p. 350.

[4] *Fabric Rolls*, Part 2, pp. 261–262.

[5] Maryanne Kowaleski, 'Taxpayers in late 14th Century Exeter: the 1377 Murage Roll', *DCNQ*, xxxiv (1978–81), pp.217–222.

receivers' rolls prior to 1343–1344, the date of the first extant Exe Bridge Wardens' account roll which is printed as Appendix II, iii, in this volume (*infra*, pp. 110–11). It is assumed that separate rolls were kept but have not survived, as the Exe Bridge estate had been established by the thirteenth century. The seal of the Exe Bridge estate is reproduced in the frontispiece and shows some of the arches of the thirteenth century bridge.

A full account of wages and prices of materials in Exeter during this period appears in Mrs Erskine's introduction to the edition of the Exeter Cathedral fabric rolls[1] and extracts of all the wages and prices for the medieval period from the Exeter receivers' rolls by the late Dr. R.C. Easterling still survive in manuscript form.[2] The receivers' rolls for the period 1304–1353 do not give wages in such great detail as the fabric rolls but the murage roll account printed in the appendix is more informative. The receiver's roll for 1339–1340 notes the payment to carpenters and sawyers at sums varying from 2¼d *per diem* including drink. In 1352–1353 three roofers and three servants were paid 7s 5d for one week with lunches (nuncheons) and two sawyers received 5d for one day's work on sawing the stocks, but with no drink.

THE CITY'S EXPENDITURE: FEES AND PENSIONS

This is one of the more predictable sections of the account rolls, at least between 1339 and 1353. The mayor's fee which was described as 60s in 1304–1305 had risen to 100s in 1339–1340 and stayed at that rate until the reign of Henry VI,[3] the total of 45s given in the 1348–1349 roll being described as the mayor's fee for three terms only.[4] The emergence of the office of receiver during the period 1304–1339 is evident by the entries on the rolls. The earlier roll records the payment of £4, i.e. £1 to each of the four seneschals. By 1339–1340 the receiver received 40s and the other three seneschals received 60s between them. The four serjeants, described as bailiffs from 1349–1350, received 36s 4d in 1304–1305 which had been raised to 40s 4d in 1339–1340 and remained at that rate until 1353 at least. The keepers of the gates received 12s (3s each) throughout the period.

It is difficult to reconcile these figures with the contemporary 'Divers Ordinances relating to the City' made on 9 October 1346 which purport to show the origin and first institution of the Common Council and the curtailing of the mayor's authority.[5] They included resolutions that the

---

[1]*Fabric Rolls*, Part 2, p. xiii *et seq*. For a table of wage rates of craftsmen and labourers 1301–1540, see John Hatcher, *Plague, Population and the English Economy 1348–1530*, London, for the Economic History Society, 1977, p. 49.

[2]DRO, unpublished notes by Dr R.C. Easterling on wages and prices in the Exeter receivers' rolls, Duryard and Exebridge accounts, 1339–1340 to 1789. The work was undertaken for Professor Beveridge's history of wages and prices.

[3]Hooker states in ECA Book 51, f. 273 that the mayor's pension was raised in 1339 (i.e. 1339–1340) from £3 to £5. The evidence for this is not known but it may indicate that no receivers' rolls in the period 1307–1338 were extant in Hooker's time, if indeed they ever existed. In ECA, Book 52, f. 504b, he states that the sum of £3 was paid from the time of 10 Henry III.

[4]There were two mayors in this year. Nicholas de Halberton died in office, presumably of the plague. (Alexander, (above, note 3, p. ix), p. 411).

[5]ECA, Miscellaneous Roll 2, no.32.

mayor's pension should be 60s, the chief bailiff's 60s, the receiver's 20s and the three other seneschals were each to receive a mark (13s 4d). Presumably these regulations, if accepted in principle, were not applied in detail as to the financial provisions.[1]

The chief bailiff (or common clerk) is paid 60s per annum in the rolls from 1339–1340 to 1347–1348 and 30s in 1348–1349. The office seems to have acquired the powers held in the city by the influential Godfrey, bailiff of the earl of Cornwall in the 1260s when the earl enjoyed an overlordship of sorts over the city. Robert de Lucy, who had held the office, evidently overreached the powers of his office in 1347 (*infra*, p. xxvii); in the 1340's he also acted as a legal adviser for the city. In 1352 for the first time the chief bailiff becomes the recorder, possibly in imitation of the practice in London, where such an official had functioned since the early fourteenth century. At first in Exeter an annual appointment seems to have been made at Michaelmas but by the end of the century it had become normal to hold office for life.

The assistant bailiff (*sub ballivus*), apparently the same as the assistant clerk (*sub clericus*) was possibly also a lawyer. John Mathu is described as holding this office between 1339 and 1348[2] and he was succeeded by Martin the clerk (Martin Battishulle).[3] There is also another clerk, the receiver's clerk but unfortunately, the receivers' rolls give little information about him and he is not named in any of the rolls in the period 1304–1353. His annual fee of 10s is listed as paid in the rolls between 1339–1340 and 1344–1345. In 1347–1348 there is a payment of 10s for 'writing and entering everything touching the usage of the community' which may indicate that the clerk was responsible for writing other documents besides the receivers' rolls. The handwriting of the receivers' rolls changes between 1344–1345 and 1347– 1348 and there are no payments to the receiver's clerk mentioned in the rolls for 1348–1349, 1349–1350 and 1350–1351.

There is a payment to the prison keeper, Richard le Gayler, of half a mark in 1344–1345 but this seems to have been a unique arrangement and may be connected with the custody of fugitives in St. John's church for which the mayor received 13s 4d for his expenses. The fees of the two attorneys retained by the city in the courts of King's Bench and Common Pleas at Westminster were 20s each per annum.

Undoubtedly the first half of the fourteenth century was a time of increasing sophistication in the city's administration. Two new offices had emerged, the receiver and the recorder. Yet the expenses on fees are very little higher in the early 1350s than in the late 1330s. If the 'Divers Ordinances' of 1346 were not carried out to the letter in achieving a reduction in the fees of the mayor, receiver and other seneschals, they may have served as a reminder to these officers that the Common Council was unlikely to look favourably on the payment of increased fees. After the sums paid as rents, the total of fees paid represented the next most costly expenditure incurred by the city and is greatly in excess of anything paid out as 'Gifts and presents' or 'Expenses and payments'.

---

[1]*Medieval Council*, p. 6, where the general provisions are discussed but not the fees.
[2]The will of John Mathu senior was proved on the mayor's court roll, 5 July 1350.
[3]Easterling, (above, note 4, p. viii), p. 409.

THE CITY'S EXPENDITURE: SERJEANTS' ALLOWANCES

Profits of the courts have been discussed in the income section (*supra*, p. xiv). Against these profits must be set the serjeants' allowances. The final totals, i.e. the Profits of the Courts minus the Serjeants' allowances, show variations from £16 to £37.

The roll for 1350–1351 is unusual in that it lists the allowances of John Chope, William Bruwere, John Large, Henry Stam and William Borne, presumably some or all of them serjeants. These allowances are described as amercements condoned by the mayor and/or other officers, some named, received from the town, and condoned because the amercements were in the fees of St Nicholas and St Stephen. In one case the amercement was condoned because the man was poor (Thomas Russel) and in another the man (Robert Polleworthy) was in the pillory. Tenants of the fees of St. Nicholas and St. Stephen were in the main exempt from the city court as the fees belonged to ecclesiastical authorities: St. Nicholas Priory and the bishop of Exeter respectively.[1] The fee of Exeter Castle belonged to the Courtenays and its tenants were similarly exempt.

THE CITY'S EXPENDITURE: GIFTS AND PRESENTS, EXPENSES (FOREIGN) AND PAYMENTS

These items are usually listed in two sections in the receivers' accounts for 1304–1353.[2] However the roll for 1348–1349 has no 'Gifts and presents' heading and that for the previous year no heading for 'Payments and expenses'. The type of entry usually expected to appear in this latter section, i.e. the *ad hoc* payments, is to be found under the 'Necessary expenses' section of the roll for 1347–1348. Although under these sections the receiver was recording foreign or extraordinary payments, many of the entries are regular payments to certain persons such as the bishop of Exeter the justices of assize, the king's collectors of taxes, the city's members of parliament and the king's messengers although the amounts differ from year to year and often take the form of bread, wine and meat. Of all the entries in the receivers' rolls it is the entries in these sections which best reflect the city's policy decisions and show the effect of national events on the city's administration.

The Black Death. It is possible that the Black Death's visitation in 1348–1349 reduced the population of England by as much as a third.[3] In Exeter 55 wills were proved on the mayor's court roll for this year, the yearly average in the previous five years being just over five. The nineteenth-century historian, Oliver, basing his account on Hooker, asserted that in Exeter we have no means of discovering the numbers that

---

[1]The tenants of St. Sidwell's fee, which belonged to the Dean and Chapter of Exeter, are mentioned elsewhere in the receivers' rolls as being free of custom but no serjeants' allowances are mentioned in respect of exemptions from fines of the city court. For a discussion of the ecclesiastical fees in Exeter *see* Muriel E. Curtis *Some Disputes between the City and Cathedral Authorities of Exeter*, Manchester, 1932, p. 11 *et seq.*

[2]Although both sections appear in the receiver's roll for 1304–1306, the entries are not detailed.

[3]Susan Reynolds *An Introduction to the History of English Medieval Towns*, London, 1982, p. 141.

perished, but that the Black Death's visitation arrested the building of the nave of Exeter Cathedral, paralysed the woollen trade and all commercial enterprise, suspended agricultural pursuits and weighed heavily in effects on the population for upwards of three years.[1] In fact the impetus of the cathedral building had slackened before 1348 and when the Black Death came the effect is not particularly perceptible in the cathedral fabric rolls.[2] The receiver's roll for 1348–1349 records the sums paid as customs as only £7 18s 3d, a considerable decrease on the sum of £23 3s 4½d collected the year before. However, the sum of £18 6s 8d was received in 1349–1350 and so it seems that trade recovered more quickly than believed by Hooker and Oliver. Obviously there was disruption in the city's government, as is evidenced by the fact that officials were paid for part of the year only but the account for the year ended with a surplus not a deficit. Under 'Foreign expenses' the receiver accounted for bread and wine for the mayor and others being out of the city at Chudleigh on various occasions. A pair of boots were given to Elias Wilde for his labour going to Chudleigh on common business (the bishop often lived at Chudleigh and the journey may have been to see him) and for the expenses of Thomas Spicer the mayor's *locum tenens*, possibly after the death of Nicholas de Halberton, the mayor who died in office. A payment of 8s 10½d to Thomas Spicer by order of the mayor, because the said Thomas was short by such an amount at the foot of his account, is also recorded on this roll.

The rents collected in 1348–1349 were only slightly down on the previous year and the profits of the courts were approximately twice the sum realised in 1347–1348. The high figure (over £15) from 'Profits of the Courts' is accounted for by income from a large number of entrants to the freedom (*supra*, p. xv) although a comparison with the mayor's court rolls reveals that only a small minority of these entries to the freedom were by succession, as might have been expected.[3] Only 16s was realised under 'Profits of Courts' for wills proved. It is difficult to explain why there were so many entrants to the freedom who were prepared to pay for the privilege of admission in a year when trade was so disrupted, unless it was because competition was stiff or perhaps because in this year the city had set its own price for admission in order to balance the books.

Royal Visits. The accounts throw light on royal visits to the city. The story that Edward III came to Exeter in 1357 on his return from France via Plymouth bringing with him John the captive king of France has been disproved.[4] In fact Edward landed at Sandwich on that occasion. The receivers' rolls, however, mention three occasions when he was expected in the the city: in 1342–1343 on his way towards France and on his return from it and in 1344–1345 on his way back from Brittany. None of these intended visits has been noticed by Exeter's historians hitherto.[5] The royal

[1] Oliver, *op cit.*, pp. 74–75.

[2] *Fabric Rolls*, part 2, pp. xxxiv–xxxv.

[3] *Exeter Freemen*, pp. 28–29.

[4] Oliver, *op.cit*, p. 73.

[5] J. Gidley, *Royal Visits to Exeter*, does not mention the proposed visits and there is no reference to them in Hooker's annals in his Commonplace Book (ECA, Book 51) under the relevant years. The visit by Queen Philippa in 1349 is noted in the cathedral accounts but there is nothing in the city receivers' accounts, presumably because she was not entertained by the city (Nicholas Orme, *Exeter Cathedral As It Was:1050–1550*, Exeter, 1986, p. 48).

DEVON & CORNWALL RECORD SOCIETY

With the Compliments of

the Hon. Secretary

7 The Close
Exeter EX1 1EZ

Mr JHK Hillenbrand

One £9 subscription

31. 5. 90

prerogative of purveyance, that is, the Crown's right of buying what was needed for the king's household at a price fixed by the purveyor (or provisioner) and of exacting the use of horses and vehicles for the king's journey, is in evidence in the receivers' rolls for the three years mentioned.

In the roll for 1342–1343 is a record of the payment to Nicholas Voysi of 22d for taking various messages to various places at the time there was discussion about the king coming through Exeter on his way to to the war in Brittany. Evidently the Welsh contingents for the war passed through the city at this time as 5s 2d was paid for 'watching and other expenses', but the king is assumed to have stayed at Dartmouth rather than Exeter on his way to France as Hugh Peaumer' is paid 10d for taking messages to Dartmouth about the coming of the king there. Edward took his army to Brittany in the autumn of 1342 and started for England after the truce of Malestroit in January 1343. The payment of 12d for a horse hired on the way to Yeovil to carry the king's saddle on its way back from Brittany and the sums listed under 'Gifts and presents' in the account roll for 1342–1343 as being paid to various messengers, to the earl of Gloucester and to the earl of Devon coming from Brittany indicate that the king was expected to return via Exeter. However, after a tempestuous voyage, which is said to have lasted five weeks, the king landed at Weymouth on 2 March 1343.[1] Evidently the fleet was dispersed, for Joan, duchess of Brittany, who is said to have accompanied the king back from France, in fact landed in Devon with her two children and stayed in Exeter throughout Lent.[2] An entry on the receiver's roll for 1342–1343 records that one carcase of beef, two pigs and six kids were sent by the city to St. Nicholas Priory where they stayed. The duchess of Brittany was famous for her gallant defence of Hennebont after her husband, John de Montfort, had been taken prisoner and she left France only after his promised release under the truce of Malestroit, on condition that he would not leave France or enter Brittany.

The receiver's roll for 1344–1345 in the 'Gifts and presents' section records payments for wine sent to the earl of Arundel's squire and the king's clerk 'for preparing victuals for the use of his said lord towards parts across the sea' (presumably the king not the earl of Arundel) and of 18s 8d given to various serjeants at arms, messengers and runners of the king. In fact the king sent the earl of Northampton with a force to Brittany and he himself embarked at Sandwich on 3 July 1345 and crossed to Sluys.[3]

The one undoubted royal visit at this time is referred to in the receiver's roll for 1347–1348 showing that Joan, the king's daughter, visited the city on her way to meet her betrothed husband, Dom Pedro of Castile. Under 'Necessary expenses' there are payments recorded for carrying one cask of wine from one place to another for the lord king's daughter going towards Spain, for a messenger hired by the city to go to Salisbury to announce the arrival of the king's daughter and for the ullage of a cask of wine sent to the king's daughter. Under 'Gifts and Presents' there are various expenses of the king's provisioners coming with the king's daughter towards Spain for her marriage, for wine, beef and pigs given to her and her officials and for

[1]*Dictionary of National Biography*, under Edward III.
[2]G.E. Cokayne, *Complete Peerage*, ed. V. Gibbs and others, X, London, 1945, pp. 820–821.
[3]*Dictionary of National Biography*, under Edward III.

TABLE 1.   TOTALS OF INCOME AND EXPENDITURE

(The arithmetic has

Year	Arrears	Fixed rents	Issues of the City (customs)	Profits of the courts	Foreign receipts	Charge (receipts) total	Rents paid	Rent deficits
1304–5	£4 10s 0d	£33 14s 3d	£29 10s 4d	£21 18s 2d	£34 0s 0d	£123 12s 9d	£25 17s 2d	£2 11s 10d
1305–6		£33 14s 3d	£33 18s 3d	£20 16s 2d		£88 8s 8d		
1339–40	£2 16s 8d	£62 19s 4d	£21 17s 6½d	£48 9s 11½d	£5 8s 6d	£141 12s 0d	£91 19s 4d	£1 11s 6d
1341–2		£11 3s 4d	£26 8s 2d	£20 3s 2½d		£57 14s 9¼d	£20 15s 5d	14s 5d
1342–3		£39 15s 7¾d	£34 11s 0½d	£22 14s 2¾d		£97 0s 11d	£51 5s 4d	£1 10s 9d
1344–5	£5 8s 4d	£41 4s 10d	£30 6s 10¼d	£24 1s 2d		£101 1s 2¼d	£51 13s 0d	£1 10s 5d
1347–8	£4 6s 8d	£37 5s 2d	£23 3s 4½d	£16 15s 11½d		£81 10s 10d	£45 17s 2d	
1348–9	£9 4s 4d	£36 14s 1d	£7 18s 3d	£32 11s 5d		£86 8s 1d	£45 17s 2d	
1349–50		£38 14s 1d	£18 6s 8d	£31 12s 5d		£91 5s 3d	£46 1s 2d	£2 11s 6d
1350–1		£38 14s 1d	£22 6s 1d	£26 15s 0d		£87 15s 2d	£46 1s 2d	£2 9s 2d
1351–2		£38 17s 1d	£19 10s 1½d	£41 5s 6¾d		£99 12s 9¼d	£23 2s 11d	£2 7s 9d
1352–3		£39 0s 10d	£24 4s 3½d	£22 14s 10d		£85 19s 11½d	£46 1s 2d	£2 8s 8d

FROM DIFFERENT SOURCES 1304–1353
not been corrected)

Rents allowed	Necessary expenses	Fees	Serjeants' allowances	Gifts and presents	(Foreign) expenses and payments	Expenses about the walls	Expenses about East Gate chapel	Discharge (expenses and payments) total
	£2 8s 5d	£16 18s 4d	14s 6d	£44 17s 7d	(£32 0s 8½d)			£124 18s 6½d
	£2 4s 3¼d	£20 10s 6d	£19 14s 6½d	£2 18s 0½d	£11 0s 4d			£149 18s 4¼d
	£1 11s 9½d	£18 13s 4d	£3 15s 11d	£3 1s 2d	£8 18s 8d			£57 10s 8½d
	13s 8d	£22 19s 5d	£2 0s 7d	£4 2s 11½d	£10 14s 11d			£93 7s 7½d
	£1 8s 9½d	£21 4s 10d	£5 2s 2¼d	£5 10s 2d	£3 17s 11d			£90 8s 3¾d
	£7 18s 6½d	£16 13s 0½d		£10 8s 11½d				£80 17s 8½d
£10 11s 4½d	£4 4s 0½d	£14 7s 8½d			£3 14s 7d			£78 19s 10½d
	£2 11s 10d	£25 6s 8d	£2 17s 10d	£1 12s 2d	£4 16s 11¼d			£85 17s 11¼d
	£4 18s 1½d	£21 9s 11d and £3 13s 4d (foreign fees)	£4 19s 4d	£2 1s 0d	£4 9s 0d and 9s 9d			£90 10s 9½d
	£1 9s 2¾d	£22 14s 3½d	£3 19s 3d	£1 2s 10d	£9 18s 9d	£1 12s 2d		£67 7s 2½d
	£1 2s 6¼d	£22 6s 4d	£2 12s 11d	11s 0d	£9 6s 11½d		12s 8d	£85 2s 2¾d

TABLE 2.   GRAPH SHOWING GENERAL LEVELS OF INCOME AND EXPENDITURE, 1304–1353

Figures are to the nearest £

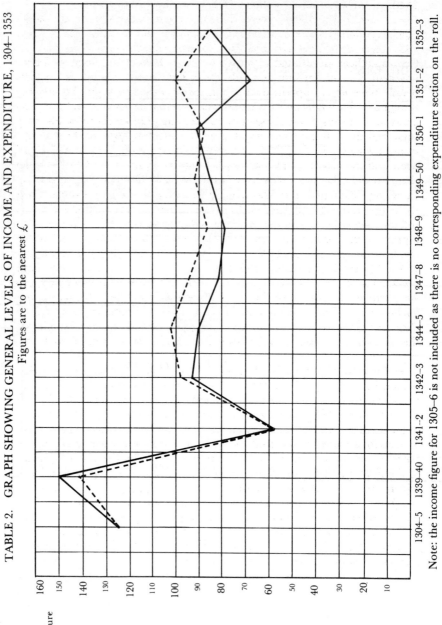

- - - income
—— expenditure

Note: the income figure for 1305–6 is not included as there is no corresponding expenditure section on the roll.

silver given to her officials. In fact Joan died at Bordeaux in September 1348, an early victim of the Black Death, on her way to Spain.

Ships and taxes. The receivers' rolls also record payments to the king's officials coming to commandeer ('arrest') ships[1] and to collect taxes. From 1334 there were new arrangements for the collection of taxes and the Crown's officers negotiated with each borough, hamlet and demesne for the payment of a certain sum as a subsidy to the Crown. Therefore the local people were left to apportion the sum to be raised as equitably as they thought fit. Boroughs and demesnes were assessed at a tenth and the rural areas at a fifteenth, but sometimes Parliament granted more or less than these and in 1338 there was an attempt to collect in kind, at the rate of a stone of wool for 2s of tax.[2] In September of the previous year, the king had been granted a tenth and a fifteenth for three years, i.e. 1338–1340 and there are references in the receiver's roll for 1339–1340 to the expenses of James de Cokyngton and Matthew de Crauthorne the king's collectors of the tenth, in the roll for 1347–1348 to the assessors of the tenths, and in the roll for 1349–1350 where they are referred to as 'taxers'. The king received a grant of the ninth sheaf, fleece and lamb from lands and a ninth of the goods of citizens and burgesses for the years 1340 and 1341 on 29 March 1340.[3] The receiver's roll for 1339–1340 mentions the collectors of the ninth and the roll for 1341–1342 records that wine and fowls of the value of 2s 10d were sent to the bishop of Exeter at Bishop's Clyst when the mayor and good men of the city came to him for counsel about the tallage of wool. The 'Necessary expenses' section of the same roll mentions candles bought for the assessors of wool, sitting in the twilight in the Guildhall solar, an evocative entry.

The new form of taxation evidently caused some problems of administration but there are few references in the receivers' rolls to the respite of taxes or to their non-payment. Two exceptions are in the roll for 1348–1349 where Geoffrey Malherbe is allowed half a mark (6s 8d) for having respite of the tenth and there is an entry for the payment of 2s to the king's serjeant at arms for an arrest made on Robert Brideport for his tenth in arrears. The bales of alum (*alym*) taken from Robert Brideport to the Guildhall by order of the mayor presumably represented a distraint on his goods. Alum was widely used in the dyeing of cloth.

The king's justices. The sums spent on the justices of assize and their officials when visiting the city represented a sizeable proportion of the 'Gifts and Presents' and 'Expenses and Payments' sections of the receivers' accounts. The gifts usually took the form of wine. The justices' session of trailbaston is mentioned in 1341–1342 when there are payments made of 13s 4d to four 'apprentices' of the law (i.e. barristers) who were attending a

---

[1]Such entries appear in the rolls for 1339–1340, 1341–1342, 1347–1348, 1348–1349 (the ship is for the earl of Lancaster), 1349–1350 ('for the prince's suit') and 1350–1351 (ships and sailors). In the roll for 1344–1345 an entry records that wine is sent to Sir Richard Cogeyn for obtaining archers for the king's service.

[2]Audrey M. Erskine *The Devonshire Lay Subsidy of 1332*, DCRS (NS vol. 14), pp. ix–x. On 28 February 1339, Richard de Novo Castro was appointed to survey the king's wool in Devon, cause it to be taken to the port of Exeter and sent to London for ship rent (*Cal. CR, 1339–41* p. 67).

[3]May McKisack *The Fourteenth Century 1307–1399*, London, 1959, p. 162.

session and for wine sent on the occasion of the two sessions of trailbaston held during the year to the justices Richard Lovel, Hamo Dyrworth, John de Sodberi, Geoffrey Gilberd and Robert Radeston. Trailbaston was a judicial commission to deal with the suppression of brigands who bludgeoned or maltreated and robbed the king's subjects during his absence or involvement in foreign wars and was instituted by an ordinance of 1304–1305.[1] Hooker mentions the ordinance under the year 1304 in his annals as 'M^d that this yere Inquisition by the King's writs were taken through the whole realm by the verdict of the most substantial men against all manner of officers that had misused themselves yn their offices by extorcions briberies or otherwise and who so were founde culpable were punished by fine or otherwise according to the offence.'[2] Unfortunately there is no evidence to suggest that this had any influence on the keeping of records in the city although the date coincides with the date of the first receiver's roll extant.

The receiver's roll for 1347–1348 includes the payment of 6s 'for the purchase of a commission for gaol delivery in which the mayor of the city was named one of the justices'. This may refer to an attempt of the mayor and of the Common Council to promote the authority of the mayor against that of Robert de Lucy, common clerk of the city, mentioned in a Commission of oyer and terminer issued in May 1347 who had been guilty of 'oppressions of the people of these parts by colour of his office.[3]

The expenses of attending Parliament. The expenses of attending Parliament on the city's behalf are also entered on the receivers' rolls, relating, for example, to Robert de Brideport and Thomas de Crauthorne in 1339–1340,[4] Philip de Bersham and Bartholomew atte Mede in 1342–1343, Simon atte Pytte and Thomas Spycer in 1351–1352. These payments were made in response to writs from the Crown, and were at the rate of 2s *per diem*, the normal rate.

CONCLUSION

Because of the short period covered by the receivers' accounts in this volume, centring upon fourteen years in the mid-fourteenth century with a foretaste given by the earliest surviving roll of 1304–1306, they are not suitable to support the broad hypotheses suggested by some historians about wealth and poverty in the late medieval towns.[5] Indeed, the preceding summary table and graph indicate after the apparent high point

---

[1] *Rotuli Parliamentorum; ut et Petitiones et Placita in Parliamento tempore Edwardi I*, vol. i, p. 178. The commission was sent to the counties of Notts., Derbys., York, Norfolk, Suffolk and Lancs. on 23 November 1304 and a second commission to other counties, including Devon, *de transgr' nominatis Trailbaston audiend' et terminand'* followed on 6 April 1305.

[2] ECA, Book 51, *sub* 1304–5 in the annals section.

[3] *Cal. PR, 1345–8*, p. 139; Hooker, in ECA Book 51 describes in 1347–1348 'a greate contention within this Cittie for and about the election of the Mayre and officers and whereof greate trobles were lyke to have ensewed had not the same benne foreseen and provyded for'.

[4] *Cal. CR, 1339–41*, p. 447 records the issue of a writ for payment to Robert de Brideport and *Matthew* de Crauthorne.

[5] A.R. Bridbury, 'English Provincial Towns in the Later Middle Ages' *The Economic History Review*, 2nd series, xxxiv (1981), pp. 1–24; Reynolds, *op.cit.*, pp. 140–146.

of 1339–1340 a steady level of Exeter's finances which is surprising in a period of disruption from plague and war, with at least one 'palace revolution' in the city itself. The apparent 'boom' year of 1339–1340 is explained largely by the arrears collected that year and not by a sudden upturn in the city's finances and prosperity. As with any series of accounts, the summary of totals does not give the whole picture, but the general level of receipts and expenditure is an important indicator of urban prosperity, especially when taken in conjunction with the Exeter customs rolls. It is unfortunate that there are few surviving accounts for other boroughs in the same period,[1] or else a comparative study on town finances could be undertaken to supplement information derived from tax assessments.[2]

The importance of the receivers' accounts lies more in the information they give on the city's history. Where the events in the rolls can be checked with other sources in the archives of the central government, such as the intended royal visits, it seems that the entries were made in chronological order. A remarkable amount of documentation exists for the period in the city archives, not least the almost complete series of mayor's court rolls, which has been researched only partially. In all these records the impression given is of a fairly sophisticated administration, efficient, and capable of creating new classes of record as need arose, as is witnessed by separate accounts for the Exe Bridge estate and the manor of Duryard. In the receivers' accounts sudden increases in costs such as the rise in the fee farm rent and the expenses of royal visits are capable of absorption without the city showing a loss at the end of the year. In only two out of the eleven years was there a small overspending: in 1339–1340 when this was caused mainly by the arrears due and in 1350–1351. The latter was rectified the following year when a large surplus is shown. Income was probably more predictable but expenditure was incurred in a variety of ways and planning must have been necessary. Payments 'by order of the mayor' and 'by order of the mayor and good men of the city' have been referred to, especially as regards the mayor's exertion of authority agains the wishes of the Common Council. If there was an administrator in charge of the accounting process it could have been the mayor, who often held office for several years running, or the receiver who in later centuries was certainly empowered to exert this authority, or the common clerk (or chief bailiff).

Like many other medieval accounts those of the receivers were not flawless in their arithmetic. Three of the totals of receipts and four of the totals of expenditure are wrong, but only with regard to shillings or pence. The accounts were audited and the auditors' names appear at the foot of the accounts from 1341–1342 onwards, but it is a modern concept that the calculations should balance exactly.[3] The arithmetic of the Barnstaple account of 1389–1390 printed as Appendix II, iv, is also wrong in the expenditure total.

---

[1]R.B. Dobson *York City Chamberlains' Account Rolls 1396–1500*, Surtees Society, cxcii (1980), p. xviii.

[2]Maurice Beresford, *New Towns of the Middle Ages*, Gloucester, 1988, p. 281; W.G. Hoskins, *Local History in England*, London, 1959, p. 176.

[3]Anthony Steel, 'Some Aspects of English Finance in the Fourteenth Century' *History*, xii (1928), pp. 299–300.

'Dark as the history of our villages may be, the history of the boroughs, is darker yet . . .' wrote F.W. Maitland 92 years ago.[1] In the case of Exeter there has been some enlightenment for the city has been fortunate in the amount of research published this century based on its exceptionally continuous series of records: for example the monographs by Dr. R.C. Easterling, Mrs F. Rose-Troup and Miss M. Curtis in the series published by the History of Exeter Research Group in the 1930s. The receivers' rolls printed in this volume are intended to shed further light on the fourteenth century; several questions as to their interpretation remain unanswered but this could be said of many financial records.

EDITING AND TRANSLATION PRACTICE

The Latin of the accounts, though grammatically accurate (errors of accidence and syntax are rare) is heavily abbreviated, and the overall impression is of a series of notes rather than an attempt at continuous narrative. The paragraphs which make up an account may consist of a single sentence made up of phrases joined by *et* or *&* (e.g.'City Rents' in Appendix I); a series of sentences each beginning with *item* (e.g. 'Rents Paid' in Appendix I); or a series of phrases without conjunctions (e.g.'Rent Deficits' in Appendix I). The only punctuation used is the full stop, which is used not only to separate entries but to divide the different components in the sums of money; no attempt has been made to reproduce this form of punctuation and all its vagaries in the transcription. The degree of abbreviation used in a given entry seems entirely arbitrary: *recept'* or *rec'*, *reddit'* or *redd'*, *acquietanc'* or *acquiet'* are used interchangeably. Only in a few cases did the receiver or his clerk consider it necessary to add more than a few words of explanation to an entry, and these longer descriptions tend, inevitably, to occur in the more miscellaneous sections on the expenditure side, such as 'Necessary Expenses' or 'Gifts and Presents'. English words are rare and do not always seem to be used where there is no Latin equivalent (e.g. *'woyf'* for the stray horse in Appendix I).

In transcribing the Latin for Appendix I it has been decided not to attempt to fill out all the contractions and abbreviations of the original, as this would serve little purpose. A number of words are left so incomplete that a decision as to whether, for example, they are singular or plural would necessarily be entirely editorial, while to lengthen the text considerably by adding putative endings to sentences liberally supplied with prepositions would add nothing to the reader's understanding of the entries. Contractions in the middle of words are a different matter, since there is often no uncertainty as to what combination of letters they represent, and these have generally been written out in full. The layout of the text has been kept in paragraphs, as in the original, rather than put into columns, as in the translation, so that the appearance of the rolls is preserved as far as possible, the main exception being that the section headings have been moved from the left-hand margin into the main body of the text.

In the translations, for ease of reference, the entries have been put into

[1] F.W. Maitland, *Domesday Book and Beyond*, Cambridge, 1897, p. 172.

columns and the marginal titles placed as headings above each section. The minimum of punctuation has been added. As much common form as possible has been omitted (e.g. expressions such as *item onerat se de* . . . at the beginning of entries), but otherwise the translation has been kept as close to the original as possible; since it is impractical to publish a complete Latin text of the accounts, it is undesirable to attempt too free a version. Sums of money have been left as they are given, except that the equivalents of marks and fractions of marks have been added in brackets. Christian names have been modernised, as have names of parishes and towns and other place names still current today (e.g. Duryard); surnames have been left as they are spelt in the original, and the names of places now either non-existent or unidentifiable (e.g. *Prattishide, Windsor, Colepole*) are printed in italics. It must be understood that the printed forms of names which contain an ambiguous n/u or c/t (e.g. Deneband, Crauthorne, Beyvyn, Screcche) are the result of an editorial decision, since it is unlikely that we shall ever know how these men were accustomed to hearing their names pronounced. Words or phrases for which no satisfactory translation has been found are quoted in italics; doubtful translations are followed by a transcription of the original in brackets; illegible or missing words are indicated by '. . .'; the titles of civic officials and words such as 'pyx', 'burgavel', and 'brithgavel' have been left in a form as close to the original as possible to avoid ambiguity.

ACKNOWLEDGEMENTS

The editors and the Council of the Devon and Cornwall Record Society are grateful to Exeter City Council for permission to publish the receivers' accounts and other Exeter documents in the appendix and to reproduce the illustrations of city seals as the frontispiece to this volume. They also wish to thank Barnstaple Town Council and the North Devon Athenaeum for permission to include the first receiver's account extant for Barnstaple in the appendix. This document and the other Barnstaple borough records are now on deposit in the North Devon Record Office. Devon is indeed fortunate in having pre–1400 receivers' accounts from two municipalities. They also wish to record their thanks to Devon County Council and to Exeter City Council for grants towards the costs of publication of this volume.

The editors wish to thank Professor Nicholas Orme for his helpful advice on the introduction and text, and Helen Mason and John Brunton of the Devon Record Office and Hugh Peskett of the Devon and Cornwall Record Society's Council for their work and guidance on the production of the computerised copy for the printer, the first volume in the Society's general series of publications to be produced by this method.

The staffs of the Devon and Exeter Institution Library, Westcountry Studies Library and Exeter Reference Library were unfailingly helpful with regard to printed sources and the staff of the Devon Record Office has borne with fortitude and tolerance discussion of the *minutiae* of medieval accounting.

Exeter,   Margery M. Rowe
August, 1989   John M. Draisey

TEXT OF THE ACCOUNTS

1304–6 (?) ACCOUNT OF ROBERT DE NYWETON', SENESCHAL OF EXETER, THE 34TH YEAR OF THE REIGN OF KING EDWARD FATHER OF THE PRESENT KING

Arrears

Arrears of the four serjeants of the preceding year		£4	10s
	Total	£4	10s

Fixed rents

Rents of Duryard		£25	12s	6d
Petty rents of the city		£8		21d
	Total	£33	14s	3d

Issues of the city

Custom of wine			51s	8d
Custom of woad and other saleable goods landed at Topsham		£4	19s	3½d
Custom of meat			66s	8d
Custom of fish		£6	6s	8d
Stephen Beyvyn for petty customs			41s	
Custom of oil			5s	
Custom of the measure of corn			5s	
Issues of the pyx for the whole year			113s	11d
Grazing sold around the town			13s	
Bagavel and brithgavel for the whole year			58s	7½d
Half of all the profits of brithgavel of the fee of St Sidwell			9s	6d
	Total	£29	10s	4d

Pleas and profits

Profits of the courts for the whole year		£11	11s	6d
Entrants to the freedom the same year		£10	6s	8d
	Total	£21	18s	2d

Foreign [receipts]

From John Gerveis for the arrears of the farm of the mill in the preceding year		£7
From the same John for the rent of the same mill in the present year and the coming year		£27
	Total	£34
	Sum total of receipts	£123 12s 9d

1

Rents paid

To the prior of Holy Trinity London for rent owed to him	£25	12s	6d
To the lord earl marshal for the farm of the city nothing this year			
To the parish chaplains of Exeter		4s	8d
Rent deficit of the house of Walter Plente			8d[1]
Door outside the East Gate			4d[1]
A gate which was formerly of William de Bikelegh			6d[1]
Total	£25	17s	2d

Rent deficits

Walter Plente's house		8d
One door outside the East Gate		4d
The gate which was formerly of William de Bikelegh		6d
The gate which Henry de Bollegh formerly archdeacon of Cornwall held with two plots which William de Pontyngton' formerly held		40d
A certain yard outside the East Gate which Stephen son of Richard le Skynnere and Robert his brother held	5s	
Fixed rent issuing from the pillory	18s	
Two shops next to the *pretorium* of the Guildhall on the west side	24s	
Total	51s	10d

Necessary expenses

Various necessary expenses of the town	48s	5d
Total	48s	5d

Fees

To the mayor for his fee for the present year		60s	
To Philip Deneband and his clerk for their fees	£3		
To the four seneschals for their fees	£4		
To the four serjeants for their fees		36s	4d
To the keepers of the gates and their signs [*signorum*] for their fees		12s	
To Robert de Boyland for his fee		20s	
To Peter Soth for his fee		20s	
To John de Peveneseye for his fee		20s	
Total	£16	8s	4d

. . .

Bread and wine bought and sent to various people for the whole year		£4	12s	9d
In various . . . to various people for a whole year . . .	£27	7s	11d
Total	£32		8½d

[1]entry crossed through

Expenses and cash payments

Various expenses, gifts and payments made	£44	17s	7d
Total	£44	17s	7d

Amercements condoned and not levied

Various amercements condoned by the mayor and seneschals		10s	
Various amercements which cannot be levied		4s	6d
Total		14s	6d
Sum total of expenses and allowances *(lib')*	£124	18s	6½d
And overspent		25s	9½d

[*Dorse*]

ACCOUNT OF ROBERT DE NEWETON, SENESCHAL OF THE CITY OF EXETER, THE *XXX* . . . ᵀᴼ YEAR OF THE REIGN OF KING EDWARD FATHER OF THE PRESENT KING

Fixed rents

Rents of Duryard	£25	12s	6d
Petty rents of the city	£8		21d
Total	£33	14s	3d

Issues of the city

Custom of wine		109s	11d
Custom of woad and other petty items landed at Topsham	£4	11s	4d
Custom of meat		66s	8d
Custom of fish	£6	6s	8d
Stephen Beyvyn for petty customs of saleable goods demised to him at farm		40s	3d
Custom of the measure of corn		5s	
Custom of oil		5s	
Issues of the pyx for the whole year	£7	14s	5d
Grazing sold around the walls of the town		13s	
Bagavel and brithgavel for the whole year		57s	6d
Half of all the profits of brithgavel of the fee of St Sidwell		8s	9d
Total	£33	18s	3d

Pleas and profits

Profits of courts for the whole year	£14	19s	6d
Entrants to the freedom the same year		116s	8d
Total	£20	16s	2d
Sum total received	£88	8s	8d

1339–40 ACCOUNT OF ROBERT DE BRIDEPORT, SPICER,
SENESCHAL AND RECEIVER OF THE COMMON
GOODS OF THE CITY OF EXETER, FROM
MICHAELMAS 13 EDWARD III TO THE SAME FEAST
IN THE FOLLOWING YEAR

Charge

Arrears received

Arrears of account of Nicholas de Godiscote receiver for the year next preceding		53s	4d
Arrears of John de Fenton for the collection of the lord king's tallage			40d
Total		56s	8d

Rents of the city

Fixed rent for the whole city and suburbs for the same time	£6	6s	4d
Farm of Duryard for the year and time of the aforesaid Nicholas [de Godiscote]	£25	12s	6d
The same farm of Duryard the present year	£25	12s	6d
Passage and house of *Prattyshide*		28s	
Bagavel and brithgavel for the same time net	£4		
Total	£62	19s	4d

Issues of the city and pasture sold

Custom of fish for the same time	£11		
Hiring out tables with trestles		41s	
Custom of meat for the same time		46s	8d
Custom of bread		6s	8d
Custom of oil		3s	
Custom of grain and flour		10s	
Custom of woad taken out of the city		2s	
Petty customs		54s	4d
Grazing sold within the North Gate and *Wyndesore*			6d
Grazing between the North and East Gates on the outside		2s[1]	
Custom of wine landed at Topsham for the same time		29s	
Custom of woad, onions and garlic and other merchandise landed there for the same time		19s	9½d
Custom of fur taken out of the city		2s	7d
Total	£21	17s	6½d

Estreats and profits of the courts

Estreats of the mayor's tourn as is shown in the serjeants' accounts	£13	14s	11d

[1]entry underlined

Estreats of courts for the same time as is shown in the serjeants' accounts	£10		22d
Amercements of the bakers		9s	10d
Fines made for the same time	£11	8s	7d
Entrants to freedom for the same time	£10	12s	8d
Issues of the pyx for the same time		22s	3½d
Goods of felons for the same time		16s	6d
One horse found as a stray (*Woyf*)			40d
Total	£48	9s	11½d

Foreign receipts

Pro loc' habendis in the Guildhall at the time of St Nicholas' fair this year		18s	
De ingress' pro vendic' porte Austral'	£10[2]		
William de Kydelond for the farm of *Crykelepitt* mill	£4	10s	
For ashes of lead sold			6d
Total		108s	6d
Sum total of the whole charge	£141	12s	

Discharge

Rents paid

To the prior and convent of Holy Trinity London as is shown by the quittance for the time of Nicholas de Godiscote receiver for the year next preceding	£25	12s	6d
To the same prior and convent as is shown by the same quittance for arrears the same year	£10		
To the same prior and convent for Easter term of the present year *viz* the 14th year as is shown by the quittance	£12	16s	3d
To the same prior and convent for Michaelmas term the same year as is shown by the quittance	£12	16s	3d
To the same prior and convent for arrears of the said rent for the said present year in full payment of all arrears of the said annual rent then owing to them as is shown by their quittance	£10		
To the receiver of the lord duke of Cornwall for the fee farm of the city *viz* for Easter term of the present year as is shown by the quittance	£10		
For Michaelmas term of the same year as is shown by another quittance	£10		
To the lord earl of Devon for one third part of the wine landed at Topsham for the same time		9s	8d
To the rectors of the city for the rent of the Guildhall		4s	8d
Total	£91	19s	4d

[2] entry crossed through

Rent deficits

William de Doune's tenement because it cannot be distrained	7s[3]	6d
William Peverel's house which William Vyke once held in *Maudelynestret'* because it has fallen down		20d[4]
One door outside the East Gate which Robert de Wotton holds for the same		4d[4]
A certain plot of Sir John Eysi opposite All Hallows Goldsmith Street lane for the same		6d
A certain lane obstructed there which the same Sir John occupies for the same	2s	
A certain gate of William de Bykeleygh now of the Friars Preachers for the same		6d
A gate which Henry Bollek' formerly archdeacon of Cornwall held for the same		2s
Two plots of land lying next to the archdeacon of Totnes's tenement which William de Puntyngdon once held for the same		16d
An exit in the back part of the same archdeacon of Totnes's tenement	2s	
A certain plot above the North Gate which the rector of St Paul's holds for the same		6d
Prior of Plympton for making a certain step in the king's street because it is being removed		4d[4]
John de Chuddeleygh's close next to the Bishop's Gate because it cannot be distrained		6d
A shop next to the Guildhall which Nicholas Coppe holds	10s	
A shop in the pillory because it is not occupied	2s	
Seeks allowance of 10s condoned of the farm of the custom of fish by the mayor and community this year	10s	
Total	31s	4d

Allowances of the serjeants

Various allowances of the serjeants as is shown in their accounts both of the mayor's tourn and of the estreats of courts *viz* of amercements condoned as is shown in their four accounts of the aforesaid tourns	£7	17s
Amercements which cannot be levied as is shown in the same accounts of the said tourns		26s 2d
Amercements to be levied for various fees as is shown in their said accounts		22s 10d
Wrong amercements[5] and other petty allowances as is shown in their same accounts of the aforesaid tourns		37s 1d

[3]*7s* crossed through
[4]entry crossed through
[5]*et sub ped' comp' cond'* written above

Amercements condoned as is shown in the four accounts of the serjeants for the estreats of all courts	£6	13d
Amercements which cannot be levied as is shown in their same accounts for the said estreats of courts	15s	5d
Amercements to be levied from various fees as is shown in their said accounts for the same estreats of courts	[no amount stated][6]	
Wrong amercements[7] and other petty allowances as is shown by the same accounts	14s	11½d
Seeks allowance of 100s with which the receiver is charged in the estreats of John de Conyngtr' for the amercements of courts which Thomas de Lytchyffeld then mayor of the city by consensus and at the request of Hamo de Dyrworth and other good men completely condoned to Edward atte Stone	100s[8]	

	Total	£19	14s	6½d

Necessary expenses

Eight dozen poplar boards for making tables at the fish market at 12d per dozen	8s	
Two dozen boards of this kind bought for the same at 16d per dozen	2s	8d
Carrying all the same boards to the Guildhall		2d
Two and a half empty barrels bought for making legs for tables		15d
1000 nails for fixing the legs to the tables and for the tables at 3d per 100	2s	6d
200 nails for the same at 4d per 100		8d
Seven small oak beams bought from John Somayst' for making trestles there at 1½d per beam		10½d
Carriage of the same to the Guildhall		1d
An oak beam of his own		4d
Hire of two carpenters hired on the Saturday before Ash Wednesday for making the tables and trestles, each taking for each day with their drink 2¾d		5½d
Hire of one carpenter for the same with his drink		3¼d
Two sawyers the same day with their drink		5½d
Hire of three carpenters for the same the Monday following, taking each of them for that day with their drink 3¼d		9¾d
Hire of three carpenters for the same day, to whom for the day with their drink 2¾d		8¼d
Two sawyers the same day with their drink		5½d

[6]entry crossed through
[7]*sub ped' comp' cond'* written above
[8]entry crossed through

The Tuesday next following for the hire of all and singular workmen as is shown particularly for the same Monday		23½d
Hire of three carpenters on the Wednesday next following for the same with their drink at 3¼d each		9¾d
One carpenter for the same day with his drink		2¾d
Two sawyers for the same day with their drink		5½d
One carpenter for the Thursday next following with his drink		3¼d
Two sawyers for the same day with their drink		5½d
One carpenter for the Friday following with his drink		3¼d
One carpenter for the Saturday following		2d
Six fotmels and seven pounds of lead bought for covering the Guildhall pentice at 2s 1d per fotmel	12s	8d
Four bundles of wood for the same		7½d
Hire of a plumber for the said lead and seven fotmels of old lead for making the said pentice and mixing it *viz* for the making of every fotmel 3d	3s	3d
His drink for the same time as the work		4d
150 nails for the same		4d
Carriage of said six fotmels from the house of Reginald Wython' to the Guildhall		1d
One lock bought for the door (*host'*) of the common chest with one hasp (*clav'*) and keys to the same		10d
Mending one lock at the South Gate		2d
Mending a house wall above the pound (*ponde'*) of the said gate		2d
One lock bought for the door of the Guildhall cellar		1d
Mending one lock for the outer door of the same cellar		1d
Two boards bought and for mending one shop in the pillory		8d
Mending the common pyx		1d
Straw for the Guildhall on occasions		4d
One lock bought for the common well of the city		1d
One key bought for the West Gate		2d
Total	44s	3¼d

Foreign expenses and payments

To Robert de Brideport attorney of the city in the bench for his concern for the city in the parliament held at Westminster in the quindene of St Hilary	6s	8d
		(½ mark)

To the same Robert for his concern there in the parliament held there in the middle of Lent	6s	8d
	(½ mark)	
To Thomas de Crauthorne for the same at that time	11s	6d
To four men for their concern there at a common council about the feast of the Assumption	36s	
To the said Robert for the same there at the parliament held there at Michaelmas	13s	4d
	(one mark)	
To Ralph Speek' for the same at that time	6s	8d
	(½ mark)	
To John de Bruton for recording one attorney for the city in the bench	6s	8d
	(½ mark)	
To Sir John de Raleygh of Beaud' then sheriff of Devon for the remaining fines for having a confirmation of the city's charter of liberties as the same sheriff had in the precept by the lord king's writ as is shown by the quittance	110s	
Paid for taking one letter of attorney of the community to the lord king's exchequer		3d
Paid for the inspection of the charter of liberties of the city at London		6d
Paid to one boy taking letters to Winchester, Salisbury and elsewhere to inspect what had been done there concerning the lord king's tallage of the ninth part etc.		8d
Paid to William de Milton for purchasing various writs against Sir William Cheyny for exoneration of a certain old debt	6s	6d
One horse hired for Alexander Oldeston riding towards Chard to the justices of assize there for carrying letters in the common business and for his expenses		16d
One horse for Simon le Taverner riding to Topsham for detaining a ship of Yarmouth (*Yernemouth*) and for his expenses there		3d
Paid to one man for carrying to London £25 12s 6d of the rents of Trinity London from the time of Nicholas de Godyscote receiver for the year next preceding		40d
Paid to one man for carrying there afterwards £10 to pay the arrears then for the same year		40d
Paid to one man for carrying to the same £25 12s 6d of the rent for the whole of the present year *viz* carrying on two occasions	6s	8d
	(½ mark)	

Total	£11	4d

Gifts and presents

Gifts and presents by order of the mayor *viz*
To the lord bishop of Exeter at Clyst on his arrival
there from the parliament held the last day of
October at London

one carcase of beef	3s	
six carcasses of mutton	3s	
six partridges		11d
six woodcock		4d
three gallons of muscadine and one quart		18d
one horse hired to carry the said presents		1½d

Bread and wine sent to Sir John de Ralegh of
Charles newly appointed sheriff of Devon   19d
Wine sent to Hamo de Dyrworth on his return from
Exeter going to court for ordinary serjeant
(*serianto ordinar'*)   6d
Bread and wine sent to the same on his first arrival
in Exeter afterwards   2s   4d
Bread and wine sent to Sir James de Cokyngton one
of the collectors of tenths of the lord king granted
for having respite therefrom   14d
Bread and wine sent to Matthew de Crauthorne the
other collector of the same tenths for the same   8d

Verte in dorso de eod' panell'
[*Dorse*]
Bread and wine sent to the sheriff of Devon having
respite from a certain writ to distrain the
community for arrears of rent of Trinity London   15d
Bread and wine sent to Sir William de Scharishill
the lord king's justice in the session of the assizes
in lent   22d
Bread and wine sent to Sir John Inge at that time   22d
Bread and wine sent to Sir James de Wodestok' at
that time   22d
Bread and wine sent to Sir Hamo de Dyrworth in
the same session   12d
Wine sent to the said Sir James de Wodestok' on his
arrival at Exeter from Cornwall afterwards   12d
Wine sent to the lord sheriff for lending help in the
first session of justices of trailbaston   12d
Wine sent to John de Stouford one of the justices of
trailbaston   6d
To the clerk of the said justices of trailbaston for
allowing the charter of liberties of the city   2s
Twelve partridges and wine sent to the lord bishop
of Exeter for having his discourse and counsel
concerning the tallage and other common business   3s   7d
Wine sent to Hamo de Dyrworth on his return from
Exeter towards court after Easter   6d

Bread and wine sent to the chief collector of the lord king's tallage of a ninth granted to him	3s	9d
Wine sent to the sheriff of Devon coming to Exeter from court		9d
Wine sent to Hamo de Dyrworth on his return towards court at Trinity term		9d
Wine sent to James de Cokyngton and Matthew de Crauthorne chief collectors of the tenth conceded to the lord king when they received the account of the south quarter of the city		10d
Bread and wine sent to Sir Thomas Crosse coming to Exeter		19d
Wine sent to Sir James de Wodestok' the lord king's justice in the session of the justices' assize in the autumn at Exeter		10d
Bread and wine sent to the same in the same session		16d
Bread and wine sent to Sir John Inge justice his colleague		16d
Wine sent to the same similarly in the same session		12d
Wine sent to Hamo de Dyrworth at the same time		12d
Wine sent to the said Sir James de Wodestok' on his arrival from Cornwall in Exeter		10d
Wine sent to Hamo de Dyrworth on his same arrival from Cornwall		10d
Wine sent to a certain Roger Norman coming to Exeter with the king's commission for acquiring ships for the lord king's navy		10d
Given to his clerk according to the ordinance of the mayor and good men of the city		40d
Bread and wine sent to the lord bishop of Exeter on the day when the good men of the city were with him at a meal according to the same ordinance	3s	
Wine sent to John de Stouford on his arrival at Exeter a little before Michaelmas		10d
To several different messagers coming to Exeter from various residences (*placeis*) of the lord king on various occasions this year	4s	
To the workers of the lord earl of Devon at Exminster by order of the mayor for drink		4d
Wine sent still to Hamo de Dyrworth on his arrival at Exeter about the feast of Michaelmas		6d
Total	58s	0½d

Fees paid and pensions

To the mayor this year for his fee	100s
To the three seneschals for their fee this year	60s
To the receiver of the city for the same	40s
To Robert de Lucy chief bailiff for the same	60s
To the subclerk for the same	20s

To the four serjeants for the same	40s	4d
To the four keepers of the gates for the same	12s	
Presents sent both to the mayor and seneschals and other good men of the town at Christmas according to the custom of the city	10s	2d
Presents sent to the same at Easter	7s	
Presents sent both to the new officers and the old ones on the election day of the new mayor and seneschals	5s	4d
To Bartholomew atte Mede the common attorney in the lord king's common bench for his pension this year	20s	
To Robert de Brideport the community's attorney in the lord king's bench for the same	20s	
To his clerk for all things touching his office for the whole year writing and for compounding his account	10s	
Parchment bought for the whole year	5s	
Ink		8d

Total	£20	10s	6d
Sum total of all expenses and payments	£149	18s	4¼d

And thus the sum total expenditure exceeds the
total receipt by £8 6s 4¼d

1341–2 ACCOUNT OF REGINALD WYTHOUN, SENESCHAL
AND RECEIVER OF THE CITY OF EXETER, FROM
MICHAELMAS 15 EDWARD III TO THE SAME FEAST IN
THE FOLLOWING YEAR

Charge

Rents of the city and the suburbs

Fixed rent for the whole city and suburbs	£6	10s	4d
Passage and house of *Pratshide*		28s	
Bagavel and brithgavel for the said time		45s	

Total	£11	3s	4d

Customs received and sold

Custom of fish and hiring out tables for the same time	£12		
Custom of meat		48s	
. . . [*hole in document*]		6s	8d
Custom of grain and flour		11s	
Custom of oil		3s	
Petty customs for the same time		54s	10d

Grazing sold for the time aforesaid			12d[1]
Custom of woad taken out of the city		2s	6d
Custom of fur taken away in the same manner		7s	
Custom of wine landed at Exmouth	£4	12s	4d
Custom of woad and other merchandise landed there for the same time		18s	3¾d[2]
Total	£26	8s	2d

Estreats and profits of the courts

Estreats of four mayor's tourns		43s	9d
Estreats of the court for the same time as is shown in the serjeants' accounts		107s	8d
Amercements of the bakers		15s	2d
Estreats of false measures for the same time		18s	9d
From entrants to the freedom for the same time	£9	. . .	
Issues of the pyx for the same time		13s	1½d
Estreats of St Nicholas' fair		24s	
Received from goods [*catall'*] of fugitives		14s	2d[3]
Total	£20	3s	2½d
Sum total of the charge	£57	14s	9¼d

Discharge

Rent deficits

William Peverel's tenement in *Maudeleynestret* because it has fallen down		20d[3]
One door outside the East Gate which Robert de Watton lately held because it cannot be distrained		4d[3]
A certain plot of Sir John Eysy opposite the church of All Hallows Goldsmith Street for the same		6d[3]
A certain lane obstructed there for the same	2s	
A certain gate formerly of William Bykelegh for the same		6d
A certain gate formerly of Henry Bollek' formerly archdeacon of Cornwall for the same	2s	
Two plots formerly of William de Puntyngdon near the site of the archdeacon of Totnes for the same		16d
A certain plot above the North Gate for the same		6d
A certain plot formerly of Henry le Carpenter at the Bishop's Gate for the same		12d[4]
A certain plot sometime of Master John de Uphavene for the same		1d

---

[1] *6d* crossed through
[2] *66s 0¼d* crossed through
[3] entry crossed through
[4] entry underlined

John de Chuddelegh's plot at the said Bishop's Gate		6d[5]
One shop next to the *pretorium* of the Guildhall		
because it is hired out for so much less this year	4s	
Shops in the pillory for the same	4s	
Total	14s	5d

Rents paid

To the petty receiver of the lord duke of Cornwall for the fee farm rent for the Easter term of the present year as is shown by quittance	£10		
To Thomas le Furbour now mayor for the rent of the said farm for Michaelmas term then next following	£9		
To the rectors of the city for the rent of the issues of the Guildhall		4s	8d
To the lord earl of Devon for one third part of the wine landed at Exmouth for the time above said		30s	9d
Total	£20	15s	5d

Allowances of the serjeants [in their accounts of the mayor's tourn]

Amercements condoned in the same as is shown in their accounts of the four tourns	7s	2d
Amercements which cannot be levied as is shown in the same accounts of the tourns	2s	9d
Amercements of the fees of St Stephen and St Nicholas and others as is shown in the same accounts of the said tourns		23d
Petty expenses made by the said serjeants as is shown in the same accounts of the aforesaid tourns		17d
Amercements condoned as is shown in the accounts of the serjeants for all estreats of court and false measures	40s	9d
Amercements which cannot be levied as is shown in the same accounts	7s	10d
Amercements of the fees of St Stephen and St Nicholas as is shown in the same accounts		3d
Petty expenses made by the said serjeants as they had in the past as is shown by the said accounts of the estreats of court and the false measures		7d
Wrong amercements as the serjeants reckon in the same accounts		15d
Amercements condoned by the mayor of the estreats of the bakers as the said serjeants reckon there	4s	8d

[5]entry crossed through

They seek allowance for the freedom of Ralph
Mazelyn because it is wrong in the roll because
there was an agreement about it for 16s[6] and the
receiver is charged with 20s[7] — 4s

In the same way for the freedom of John Jakys
skinner — 3s 4d

Total — 75s 11d

Necessary expenses

Rafters bought for making a shop in *Fleschfold*		21d
Timber bought for posts and *rybresouns* for the same		13d
Two seams of wattle for the same		4d
Spars for the same		4d
Straw for the same for thatching		8d
Wages of one carpenter for the same for three days at 3d by the day		9d
Wages of the roofer and his boy for two days 3d by the day himself with the boy		6d
Boards and trestles for the said shop		9d
Renovation of two *syth* of the Guildhall next to the pillory		2d
Mending a bench broken at St Nicholas' fair		2d
Straw to spread in the Guildhall after the said fair		1d
Repair of the Guildhall *viz*		
100 stone tiles		44d
two quarters of lime		9d
sand		3d
200 laths		8d
400 lath nails		4d
pins		1½d
wages of the roofer with a boy for five days at 4d by the day		20d
Repair of iron fire baskets *viz*:		
one quintal and three quarters of iron	8s	3d
two rafters bought for the said baskets		2d
making of the said iron with other old iron made with [*cum*] William de Crockernewill	7s	
One scale bought for weighing bread by order of the mayor		6d
One pyx bought to put the charter touching the manor of Duryard in		1d
Candles bought for the assessors of wool sitting in the twilight in the Guildhall solar		1d

[6] *16s* underlined
[7] *20s* underlined

Bread and wine and other expenses incurred at Topsham when the mayor and good men of the city searched for thieves who had stolen one little ship, by order of the mayor		20d[8]
One half mark of *numerarior'* bought		6d
Repair of a common boat at *Pratsid* in all		40d
Total	31s	9½d

Expenses and payments

To Sir Ambrose attorney of the mayor and community in the lord king's bench for his suit against the said mayor and community for £14[9] to be remitted by order of the mayor	20s	
Two casks of wine sent to the earl of Devon for his marsh at *Exilond* as he claims it was damaged by the mayor and community, by order of the mayor	106s	8d
Expenses of the mayor and good men of the city for searching for thieves at Topsham having stolen one small Picard ship		20d
To William Goos of Topsham for maintaining and binding the same thieves when they needed to be brought to Exeter		2d
To Robert atte Forde for exonerating the city in perpetuity under the account of the sheriff of the king's exchequer £6 which was in a petition in green wax by the farm of *feris* and lastage, by order of the mayor	6s [½ mark]	8d
To Sir William Pipard sheriff of Devon for delivering a boat at *Pratsid*	6s [½ mark]	8d
To four apprentices for the city who are at the justices' session of trailbaston on the morrow of the Circumcision of our Lord in the present year	13s [1 mark]	4d
To Hamo de Dyrworth's clerk for lending help in the said sessions by order of the mayor	2s	
To Hamo de Dyrworth for his pension for half a year	20s	
Expenses of two men riding to *Pratsid*, *Colpole* and Powderham and through all the port of Exmouth to detain ships for the lord king's war, by order of the mayor, in all		18d
Total	£8 18s	8d

[8]entry crossed through
[9]*£14* underlined

Gifts and presents

Various messengers for the whole year	6s	4d
Wine sent to the sheriff of Devon by order of the mayor		12d
To Hervy Tyrel then sheriff of Devon for lending help in all business touching the mayor and community, by order of the mayor	20s	
One pair of gloves offered for the same		1d
Bread and wine sent to the earl of Devon on his arrival at Exminster for his stay there, by order of the mayor		17d
Wine sent to the bishop of Exeter at Chudleigh on his arrival there about the feast of All Saints, by order of the mayor		16d
Wine sent to Sir Richard Lovel one of the justices of trailbaston coming to Exeter for the first session of the present year, by order of the mayor		8d
Wine sent to Hamo Dyrworth on his arrival at Exeter for the same		8d
Wine sent to Sir John de Sodberi at that time		8d
Wine sent to Geoffrey Gilberd at that time		8d
Wine sent to Robert Radeston at the same time		8d
Wine sent to the same justices and their officials in their second session of trailbaston in the autumn in all	2s	8d
Bastard wine sent to the earl of Devon at the Guildhall in the aforesaid first session		12d
Bastard and common wine sent to the said Hamo at his breakfast [*gentaculum suum*], by order of the mayor		8d
Wine sent to Geoffrey Gilberd on his return to court immediately after he had been admitted to the office of seneschal of the said earl, by order of the mayor		8d

Verte in dorso
[*Dorse*]

Wine sent to the same Geoffrey on his arrival at Exeter afterwards from the court		4d
Wine sent to the same at the time of the burial of the son of John de Dodisscombe, by order of the mayor		16d
Wine sent to a certain serjeant at mace by order of the mayor		8d
Wine sent to John de Ralegh of *Beaudeport* newly made sheriff		8d
Wine and fowls sent to the bishop of Exeter at Clyst when the mayor and good men of the city came to him for counsel about the tallage of wool, by order of the mayor	2s	10d

Wine sent to William Byschep one of the king's serjeants at arms, by order of the mayor		8d[?]
Wine sent to Sir Oliver de Yngham seneschal of Gascony coming to Exeter going to the lord king		16d
Wine sent to Master John de Northwode by order of the mayor		8d
Presents sent to the same when he held his entry from his chamber when the good men of the city had been with him at a meal		16d
Presents sent to all justices sitting at Exeter for taking assizes in Lent in all	5s	6d
Presents sent to the same sitting in autumn in all	3s	8d
Sweet and other wine sent to the earl of Gloucester coming to Exeter to enquire about hunters etc., by order of the mayor	2s	4d
Wine sent to Sir William Pypard newly made sheriff		8d
Wine and special expenses of the said sheriff in respect of the green wax		8d
Total	61s	2d

Fees paid

Bread and wine sent to the mayor, seneschals and other officials of the city and also to the other good men of the same city at Christmas by custom	10s	10d
Bread and wine sent in the same way at Easter	10s	10d
Wine sent to the new mayor and seneschals and similarly to the old ones on election day	3s	
Wine and fire consumed in the Guildhall on election day		13d
To the mayor for his fee for the present year	100s	
To the receiver of the city this year for his fee	40s	
To the three seneschals for the same	60s	
To Robert de Lucy chief bailiff for his fee this year	60s	
To John Mathu sub-clerk for the same	20s	
To the four serjeants of the city for their service, their offerings and their fees	40s	4d
To the four keepers of the gates for their services for the whole year	12s	
To the [receiver's] clerk for his service for a whole year	10s	
Parchment bought this year	4s	7d
Ink		8d
Total £18	13s	4d
Sum total of whole discharge £57	10s	8½d

And thus the accounts accounted and the
allowances allowed, the said receiver remains in
arrears 4s 0¾d. Thence he allows himself for
wine sent to John de Stowford 18d. And for wine
sent to the receiver of the lord duke of Cornwall
8d. Also he allows for expenses of Thomas le
Forbour and Thomas Gerveys sent to the earl of
Devon going to *Colocombe* for the common
business 15d. And thus he owes a net sum of 7¾d
which he pays on account to Robert de
Bradewohrthye now receiver of the city aforesaid.
And thus he receives quittance.

The names of the auditors of this present account:

Thomas Gerveys
Henry de Hugheton
Robert le Noble
Nicholas de Halberton

Robert de Bradeworthy
John de Sutton
Walter Whyte
William de Chageford

William de Kydelond chandler
Walter Plente
Alfred Ayleward
John Matheu clerk

1342–3 ACCOUNT OF ROBERT DE BRADEWORTHY, LATELY
SENESCHAL AND RECEIVER OF THE CITY OF
EXETER, FROM MICHAELMAS 16 EDWARD III TO
THE SAME FEAST IN THE FOLLOWING YEAR

Charge

Rent of the city with arrears

Arrears of account of Reginald Wython for the previous year			7¾d
Fixed rent issuing from the city and suburbs for the same time	£6	3s	
Passage and house at *Pratside*		28s	
Bagavel and brithgavel for the time aforesaid		43s	
Farm of Duryard	£30		
Common well			12d
Total	£39	15s	7¾d

Customs and grazing sold

Customs of fish and hiring out tables and trestles this year	£12		
Custom of meat		40s	
Custom of bread		5s[1]	
Custom of grain and flour		10s	
Custom of woad taken out of the city			40d
Custom of oil		3s	
Petty customs		56s	8d
Grazing sold			18d
Custom of wine landed at Topsham	£12	11s	
Custom of woad, iron and all other merchandise landed there for the same time	£4		6½d
Total	£34	11s	0½d

Estreats and profits of the courts

Estreats of the mayor's tourn		38s	5d
Estreats of the courts for the same time as is shown in the serjeants' accounts		71s	10d[2]
Amercements of the bakers		25s	1d
Entrants to the freedom	£9	12s	8d
Fines for having grace		42s	
Issues of St Nicholas' Fair		33s	4d
Issues of the common pyx for the aforesaid time		51s	8¾d
Total	£22	14s	2¾d
Sum total of the charge	£97		11d

Discharge

Rent deficits

One door outside the East Gate which Robert de Wotton lately held because it cannot be distrained		4d
A certain plot lately of Sir John Eysi opposite the church of All Hallows Goldsmith Street for the same		6d
A certain lane obstructed there for the same	2s	
A certain gate formerly of William Bykelegh for the same		6d
A certain gate formerly of Henry Bollek' archdeacon of Cornwall for the same	2s	
Two plots of William de Puntyndon for the same		16d
A certain plot above the North Gate for the same		6d
A certain plot formerly of Henry le Carpenter next to the Bishop's Gate for the same		12d
A certain plot of John de Chuddelegh opposite there for the same		6d

---

[1] *4s* crossed through
[2] *10d* crossed through

A certain plot formerly of Master John de Uphavene for the same		1d
The boat at *Pratside* because it was not hired out this year because it had completely deteriorated	20s	
A gate of William de Bykelegh because it cannot be distrained		6d[3]
An exit in the back part of the tenement of the archdeacon of Totnes	2s	
Total	30s	9d

Rents paid

To the seneschal of the lord duke of Cornwall for the time of Reginald Wythoun receiver for the year next preceding in full payment of the rent for Michaelmas term in the sixth [*sic*] year		24s	6d
To the same for the fee farm rent for Easter and Michaelmas terms of the present year in equal portions as is shown by quittances	£20		
To the prior of the church of Holy Trinity London this year as is shown by two quittances	£25	12s	6d
To the rectors of the city for the rent of the Guildhall		4s	8d
To the lord earl of Devon for the third part of the wine landed at the port of Topsham this year	£4	3s	8d
Total	£51	5s	4d

Allowances of the serjeants

Various allowances which the serjeants had in their accounts of the mayor's tourn	9s	5d
Various allowances which were allowed to the same serjeants above their accounts of the estreats of the courts	29s	8d
Amercements condoned to the bakers		18d
Total	40s	7d

Necessary expenses

Mending the East and South Gates in all	2s	3d
Making five pairs of iron [?] from iron in stock		12d
Repair of the pipe of the common well in all	6s	3d
Mending the fish table		4d
Mats at the Guildhall		4d
Mending the postern next to the South Gate		4d
Mending a window in the solar of the Guildhall		2d
Straw at the Guildhall		1d
Roofing at the Guildhall in all		18d
Repair of the Guildhall garden [*herbar'*]		14d
Total	13s	8d

[3]entry crossed through

Foreign expenses and payments

To Nicholas Voysi for taking various messages to various places at the time when there was discussion about the coming through Exeter of the lord king on the way to parts of Brittany, by order of the mayor		22d
Expenses at the time when the Welsh passed through the city on the way to parts of Brittany, for watching and other expenses in all	5s	2d
To Hugh Peaumer' for taking messages to Dartmouth about the coming of the lord king there on two occasions		10d
To John Parys for seizing a certain boat at Kenton because it was unloading without customs		12d
For one horse hired on the way to Yeovil [*Yevele*] to carry a certain saddle of the lord king valued at £60 coming from Brittany, by order of the mayor		12d
To Philip de Bersham and his colleague going to parliament at Westminster in the quindene of Easter on behalf of the city about the common council here in the court	10s	
To Bartholomew atte Mede for his concern there in the same parliament on behalf of the said city, for one pair of gloves		40d
For the same gloves		1d
To Robert de Lucy for his expenses in riding to the justices of measures to have respite from them	2s	
To the same justices from a fine made with them that they should not sit upon the city	60s	
To their crier	2s	
In presents sent to the same on various occasions	3s	10d
For one bushel of wheat for measuring there		7d
To Walter Whyte skinner for his expenses in riding to the bishop of Salisbury for restoring the peace between the said bishop and the community for a certain trespass committed against the same bishop's servant at the time of the burial of the earl of Devon	6s	8d [½ mark]
To three servants in the justices' session in the autumn to plead against William de Ferndon in a certain assize which the same William arraigned against the mayor and community	20s	
To the three clerks of the same serjeants	3s	
For the purchase of a certain writ of inquiry into collusion, because the said William fraudulently named the mayor and community in his writ of disagreement [*diss'*]	8s	

Expenses of the mayor and other good men of the city for the night watch for the whole session in Lent for keeping the peace by reason of a certain dispute between Sir James de Audelegh and William Chambernon'	4s	6d
Expenses of the watchers in the same manner in the sessions of the justices for taking the assize in the autumn	3s	6d
A horse hired towards *Pratside* to inspect the common boat there		3d
For the purchase of two acres of land of Matilda Oblyn which Hamo de Dirworthi holds in the manor of Duryard	10s	
To Richard le Gailler in part payment of his fee for two years for keeping the prison	7s	
For the remainder of one cask of wine sent to the earl of Devon pledged to him for the breaking of his marsh next to *Exebrigg'*	17s	
To the said Hamo for the purchase of a certain writ *de supersedendo* about the measures in the city	6s [½ mark]	8d
For one pipe bought and sent to Sir Robert Hereward for the remission of his suit against the mayor and community	33s [2½ marks]	4d
To the clerks at Exeter Castle for the late return of a certain writ for distraining suitors of the court of the city of Exeter at the suit of Sir Robert Herward		40d
Total	£10 14s	11d

Gifts and presents

To various messengers of the lord king for the whole year	5s	6d
Wine sent to Hamo de Dyrworthi on his return from Exeter going to court after Michaelmas		12d
Bread and wine sent to the earl of Devon on his coming from Brittany	6s	3d
Carriage of the same to Exminster		3d
Wine sent to the earl of Gloucester coming to Exeter	4s	6d
Wine sent to Sir Thomas Crosse		12d
Wine sent to the said Hamo on his coming from the court for Christmas		16d
Wine sent to Richard de Brankescomb justice of the measures		10d
Given to the messenger of the lord duke of Cornwall		12d

A certain present sent to the bishop of Exeter for
Christmas on his coming from the court of Rome

viz one carcass of beef bought	8s	
six carcasses of mutton	3s	6d
two carcasses of pork	6s	

For carriage of the same with one horse hired for
Alexander Oldeston to present them etc. — 6d

Cret' wine sent to Sir John Darcy and Sir Robert
Borcier — 42d

Cret' wine sent to Sir Walter Mann' — 2s 6d

Presents sent to Sir William de Shareshill and his
colleagues justices etc. in the Lent session in all — 5s 8d

One carcase of beef two pigs and six kids sent to the
lady duchess of Brittany staying at St Nicholas
[Priory] in all — 17s 2½d

Verte in dorso de eodem panell'
[*Dorse*]

Wine sent to Hamo de Dyrworth on his coming to
Cornwall after the said session — 8d

Wine sent to the sheriff's wife coming to Exeter — 6d

Bread and wine sent to the earl of Devon on the
Saturday before St Mary Magdalene — 3s 9d

Wine sent to the said Hamo on his arrival at Exeter
from court for Pentecost — 6d

Wine sent to the same Hamo on his return from
Exeter going to court before Michaelmas — 8d

Presents sent to the justices sitting on the assize in
the autumn — 6s 4d

Given to the marshal of Sir William de Shar' — 2s

Total   £4 2s 11½d

Fees and customary payments

To Sir William de Sharishill for his fee	40s	
To Robert Bemynstr' the community's attorney in the lord king's court for his fee	20s	
To Bartholomew atte Mede the community's attorney in the lord king's bench for his fee	20s	
To the mayor this year for his fee	100s	
To the receiver of the city for the same	40s	
To the other three seneschals for the same	60s	
To Robert de Lucy chief bailiff for the same	60s	
To John Mathu the sub-clerk for the same	20s	
To the four serjeants of the city for the same	40s	4d
To the four keepers of the gates for the same	12s	
To the receiver's clerk	10s	

Bread and wine sent to the mayor and other officials and the good men of the city at Christmas by custom	12s	11d
Bread and wine sent to the same at Easter	12s	11d
Wine on election day sent to the new and old officials by custom	5s	
Wine and fire consumed the same day in the Guildhall at election time		9d
Parchment bought for the whole year	4s	10d
Ink		8d

Total	£22	19s	5d
Sum total of the whole discharge	£93	7s	7½d

All accounts being accounted and allowances allowed there remains net in arrears	73s	3½d

Names of the auditors

Thomas Gerveys	Robert le Noble	Laurence Coterel
Richard Plegh	William de Halscomb	John de Colch'
Roger le Teseler'	John de Sutton	Walter Plente
Reginald Whythoun	William de Chageford	Roger de Criditone

1344–4 ACCOUNT OF JOHN DE NYWETON, MERCER, SENESCHAL AND RECEIVER OF THE CITY OF EXETER, FROM MICHAELMAS 18 EDWARD III TO THE SAME FEAST IN THE FOLLOWING YEAR

Charge

Arrears

Arrears of the account of William de Halscombe receiver for the year next preceding	55s	
Arrears of the account of Richard Plegh formerly receiver of the said city	53s	4d
Total	108s	4d

Rents

Fixed rents within the city and suburbs	£6	6s	10d
Farm of Duryard	£30		
Passage and houses at *Prattesyde*		28s	
Bagavel and brithgavel for the same time		70s	
Total	£41	4s	10d

Issues of the city

Custom of fish this year	£12		
Custom of meat		38s	
Custom of bread		5s	6d
Custom of grain and flour		6s	
Custom of woad taken out of the city		3s	4d
Custom of oil		3s	
Petty customs		50s	
Pasture sold for the same time		2s	6d
Custom of wine landed at the port of Exmouth for the same time	£6	16s	
Custom of woad iron and all other merchandise landed there for the same time		110s	4¼d
Issues of the pyx for the aforesaid time		12s	2d
Total	£30	6s	10¼d

Profits of the courts and other receipts

Issues of the four mayor's tourns		77s	9d
Four estreats of courts held there for the same time	£7	6s	3d
Estreats of the bakers for the same time		29s	8d[1]d
Fines and forfeitures for the same time		49s	6d
Entrants to the freedom for the same time	£7	5s	4d
Hiring out places at the time of St Nicholas' fair		32s	8d
John Lovecok' entering the freedom by hereditary succession of John Lovecok formerly his father[2]			5d
Total	£24		14d
Sum total of the whole charge	£100	21s	2¼d

Discharge

Rent deficits etc.

The tenement formerly of Ralph Slegh in Goldsmith Street because it stand unoccupied	10s	
A certain plot called *Hangemannesplace* for the same		6d[3]
A certain gate of Sir Henry Bollek formerly archdeacon of Cornwall because it cannot be levied	2s	
A gate formerly of William de Bykelegh for the same	2s	
Two plots which William de Pontyngdon formerly held for the same		16d
An exit from the back part of the tenement of the archdeacon of Totnes for the same	2s[4]	
A certain plot above the North Gate for the same		6d

[1] *19s* crossed through
[2] entry underlined
[3] line crossed through
[4] entry underlined

A certain shop next to the *pretorium* of the Guildhall because the rent was short by 4s	4s	
A certain plot which the subdean holds next to the entrance to his court because it cannot be levied		1d
A certain plot next to the gate of the court of the chancellor of Exeter for the same		6d
A certain plot enclosed next to the tenement of John de Chuddelegh for the same		6d[4]
The tenement of John Toiller' for the same		4d[5]
A certain plot of Roger de Troubrigg' next to the Bishop's Gate [*pot'*]		12d
A certain lane which William de Halscombe now occupies for the same	2s[6]	
The boat of *Pratsid* for the same	10s	
Total	31s	5d

Necessary expenses

Hire of one man for repairing the channel next to *Crykelpitt* within the walls		2d
Repairing one wall with plaster [*luteo*] below the South Gate		1½d
Cleaning the Guildhall in preparation for St Nicholas' fair		5d
One mat [*Nat'*] bought for the provostry [*ad P'vostr'*]		1d
Four locks and four keys newly made for one coffer to put the rolls inside in all		20d
Repairing the bridge of the South Gate		2d
Repairing tables and trestles at the fishmarket in all		15d
To Roger de Troubrygg' for the construction of one door [*valve*] newly made at the South Gate with planking of the bridge there and planking at the bridge of the East Gate *viz* in timber and iron at piece work [*ad tax'*]	4s	9d
Hire of two men to build one wall below the conduit at the quarry [*Quarr'*] on piece work	2s	
For one lock and one key for the door [*valv'*] of the West Gate		10d
Mending and repair about the roof of the whole Guildhall:		
eight quarters of lime price per quarter 5d		40d
24 deams of sand *viz* three seams for 1d		8d
2000 stone tiles price per 1000 16d	2s	8d
1000 laths		40d
3000 pins		3d
3000 lath-nails price per 1000 10d	2s	6d
spiking for fixing two bosses above the solar of the Guildhall and repair of the same bosses		6d

[4] entry underlined
[5] line crossed through
[6] entry underlined

hire of one roofer with a boy for the same work
for two whole weeks *viz* 4½d a day with their
drink   4s   1d
for half their allowance   2d

                                               Total   28s   9½d

Foreign expenses
For the clerk of Master Richard de Chuddelegh for
writing an appeal on behalf of the community
against the dean and chapter of Exeter   6d
To a certain notary for making certain instruments
between the said dean and chapter and the
mayor and community about the ways and paths
of the cemetery of the church of St Peter at
Exeter by order of the mayor   2s
Expenses about men working and guarding fugitive
felons at the church of St John the Baptist in all   11d
To Robert le Noble and Vincent Squyer riding to
London for carrying and bringing [to court]
records and processes between John le Cok spicer
and Beatrice Beauson   18s
Paid for weights and a box [*fur'*] for the same and
repair of one balance   6d
To William le Tayllor of Teignmouth for having
two quittances from his hand for a certain annual
pension of 20s granted to Sir Ambrose of
Nyweburgh *viz* for two years outstanding by
order of the mayor   13s   4d
To John Matheu in part payment of 20s granted to
him from a clear [*mera*] gift of the mayor and
community   6s   8d
                                                             [½ mark]

To the bailiff of the hundred of Budleigh for
amercement of the mayor and community at the
suit of Richard le Arblaster   6d
Expenses for the delivery of ten pounds to the
exchequer of the lord duke of Cornwall at
Westminster   13s   4d
For obtaining quittance from it   2s
To Master William Criour the advocate of the
mayor and community against the dean and
chapter at the time of the reconsecration of the
cemetery etc.   40d
To Master Robert Peek registrar of the consistory
for showing favour in the same cause   3s
For carrying various letters to Hamo de Dyreworthi
at London and Bartholomew att' Mede and
others for arranging the admission of records and
processes between John le Cook spicer and
Beatrice his sister   18d

To the mayor for his expenses made by day and
    night about the custody of fugitives at the church
    of St John the Baptist for the whole time when
    they were there in all   13s   4d

                                        Total   77s   11d

Gifts and presents

Wine sent to the bishop of Exeter coming to Exeter
    to reconsecrate the cemetery   3s   10d
Wine sent to the wife of William Chaumbernoun by
    order of the mayor   8d
Wine sent to John de Ralegh of *Beaudeport* on the
    day when he drew the agreement between himself
    and Thomas le Fourbour   10d
Bread and wine sent to Walter de Horton sheriff for
    showing favour on the account of the green wax   15d
Bread and wine sent to Sir John de Cheverston
    newly made sheriff of Devon   2s   5d
Wine sent to Sir James de Cokyngton the chief
    collector of tenths and fifteenths for the present
    year   8d
Wine sent to William de Ferrers of *Churcheton*
    colleague of the said James   8d
Wine sent to Hamo de Direworth at his arrival
    from court for Christmas   20d
Wine sent to Master Richard de Chuddelegh for
    having counsel against the dean of Exeter for the
    cemetery   4d
Bread and wine sent to Sir William de Cusaunce,
    Hugh de Berwyk' and John Daberoun coming to
    Exeter on the way to Cornwall   40d
Bread and wine sent to Hamo de Dirworth and the
    other justices of the lord king and the serjeants
    sitting in the session of assize in Lent in all   7s   7d
Wine sent to James de Cokyngton receiver of tallage
    of the lord king this year   4d
Wine sent to William de Cusaunce and Hugh de
    Berwyk' coming to Exeter from Cornwall at the
    house of John de Sutton   16d
Wine sent to John Moneroun at the house of Walter
    Unyng at that time   8d
Wine sent to Sir Hugh de Nevyle knight on the day
    when the mayor and good men of the town were
    with him at a meal   16d
Canonical bread and wine sent to the bishop of
    Exeter when he held a meal with the aforesaid
    brothers   4s   4d
Wine sent to Sir Richard Cogeyn knight coming to
    Exeter for obtaining archers from Exeter for the
    service of the lord king   8d

Given to one squire of his for giving help towards [erga] his master therein	2s	
Wine sent to a certain squire of the lord earl of Arundel coming with one clerk of the lord king for preparing victuals for the use of his said lord towards parts across the sea		8d
Wine sent to John Moneroun coming to Exeter for having the fee farm rent for Easter term this year		8d
Wine sent to John Daberoun by order of the mayor		8d
Wine sent to the son of William Gyrard of Bordeaux at the house of Nicholas Trota by order of the mayor		8d
Wine sent to a certain serjeant at arms of the lord king coming to Exeter from Brittany		8d
Wine sent to Geoffrey Gilberd about Lammas day		8d
Given to a clerk of Sir William de Cusaunce for purchasing a writ of discharge against the lord king from £160 which ran upon the city for want of making a writ of access to the lord duke of Cornwall		40d

Verte in dorso
[Dorse]

Bread and wine sent to the justices and serjeants and apprentices in the justices' sessions in autumn in all	8s	1d
Given to Affeton the justices' crier etc.		12d
Bread and white wine price 6d a gallon and partridges bought and sent to the lord bishop of Exeter at his arrival at Clyst from Chudleigh	5s	2d
Wine sent to Hamo de Direworth during his stay at Exeter after the assizes in autumn		12d
Wine sent viz two gallons to one serjeant at mace by order of the mayor		12d
One pipe of wine given to Hamo de Dirworth for giving help against the justices of the lord king for admitting records touching John le Cok' spicer with two suitors price	28s	
One breakfast held about John Daberoun and others who are with the duke of Cornwall in the presence of the mayor	2s	4d
Given to various serjeants at arms of the lord king and various messengers of the lord king and runners in all	18s	8d
One lamprey bought and sent to the bishop of Exeter at Chudleigh	40s	
One pannier to carry the same		1d
Canvas to wrap the same		2d
To a certain carrier of this present		2d
Total	110s	2d

Allowances of the serjeants

Various amercements condoned and which cannot be levied and all other allowances as is shown in the serjeants' accounts *viz* of the mayor's tourn	25s	9¾d
Amercements condoned and which cannot be levied and of all other allowances as appears in the accounts of the said serjeants *viz* of estreats of court	71s	4½d
Customs of Robert Lambyn of Winchelsea which he put with the receiver in the name of a pledge who was afterwards found to be a freeman of the liberty of Winchelsea	4s	
For a certain man in the freedom of Hampton in which John Chivaler received		12d
Total	102s	2¼d

Rents paid

To the prior and convent of Holy Trinity London for their annual rent	£25	12s	6d
To the lord prince and duke of Cornwall for the fee farm rent of the city etc. as is shown by quittance	£20		
To the rectors of the city of Exeter for rent owed to them for the Guildhall		4s	8d
To the earl of Devon for a third part of the wine landed at the port of Exmouth for the time as below etc.		45s	4d
To Robert de Brideport lately receiver of the aforesaid city for his excesses as is shown at the foot of his last account of his aforesaid office		70s	6d
Total	£51	13s	

Payment of fees and pensions and customary payments

To the mayor for his fee	100s	
To the receiver of the present year for the same	40s	
To the three seneschals for their fees for the same year	60s	
To Robert de Lucy for his pension for the same year	60s	
To the sub-clerk for the same	20s	
To the four serjeants of the said city	40s	4d
To the four keepers of the gates of the same city for the same	12s	
Bread and wine sent to the mayor and the other officials and good men of the said city at Christmas according to the custom of the same city	11s	11d
Bread and wine sent to the same at Easter as of custom etc.	11s	2d

Wine sent to the new and old officers on election day etc.		5s	
Wine and fire consumed in the Guildhall on the day of the same election			13d
To Robert de Bymynstr' attorney of the city in the lord king's bench for his pension this year		20s	
To Richard le Gayler for his pension this year for guarding the prison [*prisonis*] of the city		6s	8d
		[½ mark]	
To Bartholomew atte Mede attorney of the mayor and community in the lord king's common bench		20s	
To his clerk for writing and executing all his business touching his said office		10s	
For parchment		6s	
Ink			8d

Total	£21	4s	10d

Sum total of the whole discharge	£90	8s	3¾d

And all accounts accounted and allowances allowed the total of the charge exceeds the total of the discharge by £10 12s 10½d which remains in arrears.

And the names of the auditors are

Henry de Hugheton mayor	John Toillere	John de Colebrok' skinner
Thomas Gerveys	John de Sutton	William de Chageford
Thomas le Forbour	Nicholas de Godiscote	Robert Toyllere
Richard Plegh	Walter Whyte	John Davy junior
Robert de Brideport	John Gyst	John Mathu clerk
Roger de Teseler	John Whyte	Richard Olyver

And he finds pledges to pay the aforesaid sum *viz*

John Gyst	Robert Toillere
John Whyte	John Davy junior

1347–8 ACCOUNT OF THOMAS LE SPICER, SENESCHAL AND RECEIVER OF THE COMMON GOODS OF THE CITY OF EXETER, FROM MICHAELMAS 21 EDWARD III TO THE SAME FEAST IN THE FOLLOWING YEAR

Arrears

Arrears of Nicholas de Halberton lately receiver of the common goods of the same city	63s	4d
Arrears of John Gyst lately receiver of the common goods of the same city	24s	

Total	£4	6s	4d

Fixed rents

Fixed rents of the whole city and suburbs for the aforesaid time as is shown in a schedule attached to the present account		77s	6d
Passage of *Prattesside*		7s	8d
Bagavel and brithgavel of the whole city and suburbs for the aforesaid time		60s	
Farm of Duryard for the aforesaid year	£30		
Total	£37	5s	2d

Issues of the city

Grazing sold inside and outside the city walls for the same time		2s	
Custom of fish for the same time	£12		
Custom of meat for the same time		45s	
Petty customs for the same time		30s	
Custom of flour		2s[1]	
Issues of the pyx this year		9s	5d
Custom of wine landed in the port of the aforesaid town for the aforesaid time	£4	12s	8d
Custom of iron and various other merchandise landing there for the same time		33s	11½d
Custom of woad this year		5s	
Total	£23	3s	4½d

Profits of the courts

Profits of the courts and the mayor's tourn for the same time as is shown by the serjeants' accounts		57s	8½d
From entrants to the freedom for the same time as is shown in the roll	£7	18s	8d
Amercements of the bakers for the aforesaid time		28s	6d
Customs of St Nicholas' fair for the said year		50s	1d
For fines and redemption fees of various men for the whole of the aforesaid time		41s	
Total	£16	15s	11½d
Sum total of all receipts	£81	10s	10d[2]

Rents paid

To Robert atte Cok' and John Daberoun for two quittances of rents of the farm of the town of Exeter at two terms of the year *viz* Easter and Michaelmas for the aforesaid year	£20

[1] *And no more because 4s 8d in the hands of William Stockelegh executor of the will of Walter White paid on account 3s 4d and the residue is condoned by the mayor* written above
[2] *£80 30s* crossed through

To the parish chaplains of the city of Exeter at the two terms of the year for the rent of the Guildhall of Exeter		4s	8d
To the prior of Holy Trinity London for the rent of Holy Trinity of the same place for the aforesaid year paid there by the hand of Hamo de Dereworth	£25	12s	6d
Total	£45	17s	2d

Necessary expenses

Parchment bought		12d
Mats bought for the bench [*scannum*] of the Guildhall		5d
Parchment bought otherwise		4d
Solder [*sandura*] and making lead on the East Gate		20d
Making new boards and trestles and for mending the old trestles	5s	
Parchment bought for this		10d
Mending the Guildhall solar in various places	2s	
For the mayor's expenses riding to Chudleigh on various occasions on the common business		4d
For making two keys for the Guildhall cellar and making one . . . [*illegible*] and one *Plour* and for mending one lock of the postern outside the South Gate		12d
For making benches of the Guildhall after the feast of St Nicholas		3d
For making one stall about the pillory [*collistregium*]		5d
For wine drunk to seize a cask of Robert de Bradeworth'		4d
For bringing in and taking out the said cask in the Guildhall and outside		4d
For wine given at the mayor's house		3d
For wine given to the collector of the fifteenth		2½d
For the expenses of the bailiff of Winkleigh for saving our liberty		4d
For delivering a box from the house of William de Halscomb to the Guildhall		1d
For delivering the stocks from the Guildhall cellar into the Guildhall		1d
For straw bought for the solar at the time of the tax of the tenth		1d
For carrying one cask of wine from one place to another for Joan the lord king's daughter going towards Spain		3d
For one carpenter hired for mending the said cask		2d

For a certain messenger hired by the city to go to Salisbury to announce the arrival of the king's daughter	2s	
For the purchase of a commission for the justices' assize for the prisoners of the city of Exeter	2s	
For silver [*argent'*] given to John Forlang and his colleague for the purchase of the said commission		12d
For ullage of a cask of wine sent to the king's daughter	5s	6½d
For a certain agreement [?fine] made for having the lord king's licence for a certain summons which is called a pipe	13s	4d]
	[one mark]	
For the goods of William Chamberleyn a felon for fines and forfeit goods before William de Schareshall and his colleagues paid to the sheriff	6s	8d
	[½ mark]	
For making a certain cask		4d
Parchment bought		10d
For mending a lock at John de Stoford's house		8d
For wine given to the taxers of the amercements of the courts held in Michaelmas quarter		3d
To a certain clerk writing a writ of parliament		1d
For wine given to the chief collectors of the tenth		2d
For the expenses of Thomas Spycere riding to parliament for having discourse [*de colloquio habendo*] with the lord prince	3s	9d
For two pairs of shackles for guarding the prisoners		16d
For merchandise bought for the whole year	8s	
For expenses and the purchase of the election writ for Exeter		18d
For purchase of a commission for gaol delivery in which the mayor of the city was named one of the justices	6s	
For the expenses and the work of the same Thomas and his colleagues in the same parliament and in the purchase of the same writs	£4 4s	
To a certain boy delivering to Lady Katherine de Montacute		1d
Parchment bought	2s	
For work on the Guildhall	3s	8d
For wood for a bench at the mayor's election		3d
For wine drunk by the mayor and other good men making enquiry touching the house of St Mary Magdalene		7½d
For wine and fire bought on the mayor's election day		12d
For wine bought and sent to the new officers and the old the same day	5s	5d

Total £7 18s 6½d

[*Dorse*]

Fees

To the mayor for his fee this year	100s	
To Thomas le Spicere seneschal and receiver	40s	
To John de . . . seneschal	13s	4d
To John de Bynlegh seneschal	13s	4d
To John de Nyweton mercer seneschal	13s	4d
For the fee of Robert Lucy chief bailiff	60s	
For the fee of John Mathu his clerk	20s	
For the fees of two serjeants for the same time	20s	
For the fees of the four keepers of the gates of the town for the same time	12s	
For his clerk writing and entering everything touching the usage of the community in his paper for the same time	10s	
For the fee of John Toyllero this year	20s	
For bread and wine sent to the mayor and other good men according to the custom of the city at Christmas	17s	2½d
For bread and wine sent to the mayor and other good men according to the custom of the city at Easter	13s	8d
Total £16	13s	0½d

Gifts and presents

Bread and wine sent to Henry de Baa the king's serjeant at arms		8d
Wine sent to the lord bishop of Exeter on his arrival from London on the Friday after the feast of St Luke the Evangelist	2s	2d
Wine sent to Sir Hugh Courtenay the lord earl's son	2s	
Wine sent to the sheriff of Devon		12d
White muscadine wine sent to the lord bishop at Chudleigh on All Saints' Day with the hire of a horse	2s	3d
Silver given to a certain messenger of the lord king carrying a writ for parliament		12d
Silver given to a certain messenger carrying a writ for discharging men of the city		6d
For the expenses of the provisioners of the lord king coming with the said lord king's daughter towards Spain for her marriage		18½d
Wine sent to Sir Ralph de Bedyngton knight		20d
Wine sent to Sir Adam de Schareshill knight		10d
For the expenses of the provisioners of the lord king for his daughter still coming towards the parts of Spain		12d
Silver given to the said provisioner for not taking victuals in the city	6s	8d
		[½ mark]

Silver given to two messengers of the lord king's exchequer		6d
Silver given to the rector of the church of St Pancras in Exeter for asking [*rogand'*] of the mayor and community since the Guildhall is the same parish as the church	2s	
Silver given to John Forlang' and his colleague		4d
Wine given to the assessors of the tenth part of the city		5d
Wine given to the sheriff and the provisioners of the king's daughter		7½d
Wine given otherwise to the sheriff and provisioners in the presence of the mayor by order of the same	2s	6½d
One cask of wine sent to Lady Joan the lord king's daughter	63s	4d
Cretan wine sent to the same Joan	2s	
Two carcasses of beef to the same	18s	
Four pigs sent to the same	13s	1d
Bread and wine sent to a soldier coming from Spain with the said lady	2s	2d
Wine given to various officials of the said lady on various occasions		9d
Silver given to Sir Thomas de Dudly the treasurer of the said lady with one pair of gloves	13s	5d
Silver given to various officials of the aforesaid Lady Joan	9s	2d
Wine yet again given to the aforesaid officials of the aforesaid lady at the mayor's house on various occasions	2s	
Bread and wine given to the justices and serjeants for taking the assize in Lent and also to the newly made sheriff	10s	8d
Wine given to the archers coming to the lord king's daughter going to Plymouth	2s	
Wine sent to Sir Alan de Aysche baron of the lord king's exchequer		8d
Wine sent to a certain serjeant of the lord king		8d
Wine sent to Hamo de Dereworth and Adam[3] Bry' justices assigned to deliver the gaol of the city of Exeter		16½d
Wine sent to Robert de Cok' receiver of the lord prince	4s	
Wine sent to Sir William de Schareshill on his arrival at Exeter on the Saturday in the eve of Pentecost to take the assizes between John de Thoriton and Edward Cortenay on two occasions	2s	8d
Wine sent to Hamo de Dereworth on his arrival on the next day as above		8½d

[3]*Robert* crossed through

Wine sent to Sir William de Schareshill on his
arrival from Cornwall   3s

For the expenses of William Spaldyngh the king's
serjeant coming to arrest ships   12½d

For the expenses of William Mynycch' and John
Math' junior riding towards *Prattishide*, Kenton
and Topsham for arresting ships, with the hire of
horses   12d

A gift given to three messengers of the lord king's
exchequer   6d

Wine sent to William Weston and William
Spaldyngh serjeants of the lord king   6d

Wine given at the house of Nicholas de Halberton
for 28s from the same of having custom   2d

Wine given of the custom of fish for having their
custom for the term of the Nativity of St John the
Baptist   4d

For the expenses of William Roke attorney of
Robert de Bek' coming for money owed to the
said lord prince for the fee farm of the aforesaid
city for Easter term   5d

Silver given to a certain clerk for writing letters of
the mayor and community touching Spaldyng'
the lord king's serjeant   6d

Wine drunk at the cellar when the said Spaldyng
attached the aforesaid mayor   3d

Wine sent to Robert Bek'   8d

Wine sent to one of the king's serjeants coming from
Brittany   4d

Wine sent to Master Nicholas Terrier   8d

For the expenses of John de Bynlegh, John Mathu,
Alexander Oldiston and others riding at
Prattisside to arrest a ship with corn unloading
without a licence   2s   1½d

Wine sent to Walter de Henlegh the lord king's
serjeant   8d

White and red wine sent to William Spaldyng the
lord king's serjeant   9d

Bread sent to the same William at the same time   9d

Oats and bread sent for horses to the same on the
same occasion   14d

Wine sent to the sheriff of Devon   8d

Wine sent to Lady Katherine de Montacute   2s

Wine sent to Sir John de St Paul   2s

Wine sent to Sir John de St Paul on his arrival from
London   2s

Wine sent to Grene and Thorp serjeants for the
assize of the lord king in the autumn   2s

Wine sent to Adam[4] Bryt at the same time   12d

[4]*Ralph* crossed out

Wine sent to James Huse at the same time			12d
Bread and wine sent to Hamo de Dereworth at the same time			19d
Wine sent to Alan de Aysch baron of the lord king's Exchequer at the same time			12d
Wine sent to Sir Thomas de Crosse at the same time			12d
Wine given to two messengers carrying a writ for the collection of the tenth			4d
Money given to the same messengers		2s	
Wine sent to Sir Peter de Gildisburg' on two occasions			18d
Wine sent to Hamo de Dereworth for receiving the payment of the residue of the farm of Duryard			12d
Wine given to Thomas de Hacheway by order of the mayor at the house of Nicholas de Halberton			5d
Wine sent to Sir John de St Paul on his arrival from Cornwall			22d
Silver given to a certain messenger carrying news of Treng'			3d
Silver given to Yerlyng and his colleague messengers of the lord king		4s	

Total	£10	8s	11½d
Sum of all expenses	£80	17s	8½d
The sum total of all sums received	£81	10s	10d

Of which he accounts in payments, rents, fees of
officers and all other expenses £80 17s 8½d. And
thus the sum of receipts exceeds the sum of
payments and expenses by 13s 1½d.

Afterwards he allows to the same 2s for grazing
within the walls of the city which he did not
receive. And thus he owes 11s 1½d. He seeks an
allowance of 20s in aid of his fee which is respited
until etc., and thus allowed to the same.

The names of the auditors of the aforesaid account

Robert Nobel mayor	John Brounewille
John Gyst	Roger de Criditon'
Roger atte Wille	Richard Oliver
Adam Lydyard	John Sleghe

The aforesaid accountant also declares on oath the
additions and subtractions in his present account
as far as the addition or subtraction can be shown
to be rightly done.

1348–9 ACCOUNT OF JOHN GYST, SENESCHAL AND
RECEIVER OF THE COMMON GOODS OF THE CITY
OF EXETER, FROM THE MONDAY AFTER THE
ANNUNCIATION 22 EDWARD III TO MICHAELMAS IN
THE SAME YEAR

Arrears

Arrears of John Wyta receiver of the common goods of the said city from Michaelmas last to the aforesaid Monday as is shown by the account of the aforesaid John Wyta	£9	4s	4d
Total	£9	4s	4d

Fixed rents

Rents of the aforesaid city both in the city and in the suburbs of the same city for the whole year with the rent of one messuage of *Pratteshyde*	£6	14s	1d
Nothing from the passage because the boat is completely broken and will be repaired in the future[1]			
Rent of the farm of Duryard	£30		
Total	£36	14s	1d

Issues of the city

Custom of fish from Christmas to Michaelmas	£4	6s	8d
Custom of meat from Easter to Michaelmas		16s	
Custom of flour for half a year			6d
Issues of the pyx from Michaelmas to Michaelmas		36s	10d
Custom of wine for the same		9s	10½d
Custom of iron and other merchandise for the same time		6s	10½d
Petty farms as is shown by the rolls of the courts			18d
Nothing for grazing and custom of woad			
Total	£7	18s	3d

Profits of the courts

Amercements of courts and mayor's tourns for the whole year because the estreats from them were not delivered to the bailiffs before Easter	£12	5s	4d[2]
Entrants to the freedom for the same time as is shown by the roll of the court, and not more because Richard Goldsmith, John Holle and John de Beridone have entered the freedom and have as yet not paid the fine	£15[3]		
Amercements of the bakers for the same time		8s	6d

---

[1] entry written above the line
[2] *£8 4s 6d* crossed through
[3] £12 6s 8d crossed through; above line *6s 8d* crossed through *because an error*

Fees of Robert de Lucy for wills proved for five weeks		16s	
Bagavel and brithgavel for the same time		23s	7d
Fines and waif cattle for the same time and strays		58s	
Total	£32	11s	5d
Sum total of the whole charge	£86	8s	1d

Rents paid

To John Conyng' receiver of Lord Edward prince of Wales and duke of Cornwall for the rent of the farm of the city of Exeter for Easter and Michaelmas terms for the aforesaid year	£20		
To the prior of Holy Trinity London for the rent of the aforesaid city for Easter and Michaelmas terms as is shown by two quittances	£25	12s	6d
Paid to the parish rectors[4] of the aforesaid city at the two terms of the year by custom called ancient rent		4s	8d
Total	£45	17s	2d

Fees paid

To Robert Noble for his fee from Monday before Epiphany in the 22nd year to Michaelmas next following *viz* for three terms		45s[5]	
To John seneschal and receiver		20s[6]	
To Adam Lydyurd senschal, Roger atte Wille and John Brounewille seneschals for their fees this year		36s	8d[7]
To William Wyke chief bailiff		30s	
To Martin the clerk		20s	
To the three serjeants for their fees for one half year		15s	1½d
To Master Thomas de Forsdone for his serjeant's fee for a whole year		10s	1d
To Nicholas Wytyng, for his fee		20s	
To Robert Bymystre attorney of the mayor and community at the lord King's bench in part payment of his fee		20s	
To Nicholas Trot' for his fee for one quarter		15s	
To Roger de Critton for his fee		6s	8d
		[½ mark]	
Bread and wine sent to the mayor, seneschals and other officers on Easter Eve according to the custom of the city		16s	6d[8]

[4] *chaplains* crossed through
[5] *75s* crossed through
[6] *30s* crossed through
[7] *40s* crossed through
[8] *14s* crossed through

To the four keepers of the gates of the aforesaid city
for two terms   6s
To John Fraunceys for his fee   26s   8d

| | Total | £14 | 7s | 8½d |

Necessary expenses

To Nicholas Wytyng' and Robert Crauthorne for
their expenses at parliament at Westminster   40s
To William Hynelonde attorney of John Cory for
the work of the said John which was promised to
discharge the said city from a certain sum of
money £67 which was exacted annually by the
earl of Devon in the pipe [roll] for the farm of the
same city in arrears   13s   4d
To the clerks of the prince of Wales for their fee for
two quittances by custom   4s
To a certain roofer for roofing the Guildhall of
Exeter for the next week after Sunday in the
middle of Lent for him and his two colleagues   2s   6½d
Wedges [*cavill'*] bought   4d
Roofing stones bought for the same   18d
Nails and laths   6d
To the said roofers and two boys for the week then
next following   2s   6d
To the said roofer and his boys for three weeks   2s   6d
One lock for the door of the chest below the pillory   2d
Parchment bought for the rolls of the courts and
other material for the whole half year   3s
Ink bought from Christmas to Michaelmas   6d
To his clerk writing and entering his account and
all other things in his papers for the aforesaid time   10s
One quarter of lime bought for the aforesaid roofing
of the said hall   14d
To Thomas de Forsedone for his fee on Easter Eve
because he was not at home   6d
To the other bailiffs   18d

| | Total | £4 | 4s | 0½d |

[*Dorse*]
City of Exeter, Account of John Gyst, Receiver, 22 Edward III

Foreign expenses

To a certain messenger of the lord king by order of
the mayor   . . .
For expenses *viz* for bread . . . of the mayor and
seneschals being at Chudleigh on Easter Eve for
common business against William Sleghe   10d
Expenses of the same mayor, seneschals and others
at Exeter at . . . the same day   4s   9½d

A pottle of wine given to Richard Gyffard being at Chudleigh for common business and for his horse		4d
To Nicholas Wytyng for his labour at Chudleigh for common business on various occasions	6s	8d
To Richard Gyffard for common business at Chudleigh		8d
Offerings at Polsloe on the day when they rode by order of the mayor		. . .⁹
One gallon of wine to the same mayor and other officers		8d¹⁰
Two gallons of wine sent to the serjeants at arms of the lord king and the prince's housekeeper coming to receive a certain sum of money from the collectors of the county of Devon		16d
One pottle of wine given to the same on another occasion		4d
To a certain messenger of the lord king by order of Thomas Spicer the mayor's *locum tenens*		6d
Two gallons of wine sent to Walter de Wodelonde		16d
To Geoffrey Malherbe for having respite of the tenth of the lord king existing heretofore	6s	8d
	[½ mark]	
To a certain messenger of the lord king by order of the mayor		6d
To Robert Broun and Roger atte Wille for seizing a certain horse straying [*strayur'*] for one pottle of wine		4d
Bread and wine sent to Guy [*Gwydone*] Brian by order of the mayor	3s	9d
To a certain messenger of the lord king coming with the said Guy		6d
To the messenger of the earl of Lancaster	2s	
One hat [*capella*] bought and given to Nicholas Wytyng by order of the mayor		12d¹¹
One pottle of wine given to Elias Tremenet and his colleagues jurors at the session before Sir John de Schareshulle and his colleagues		4d
To a certain messenger going to Plymouth with various men of the lord king sent to the earl of Lancaster		6d
To a certain serjeant at arms of the lord king for an arrest made on Robert Brideport for his tenth in arrears	2s	
To the sheriff as a gift	13s	4d
To a certain messenger by order of the mayor		3d

⁹*3s 4d* crossed through
¹⁰*8d* crossed through
¹¹*12d* crossed through

To the bailiffs and other men carrying bales of alum [*Alym*] to Exeter Guildhall taken from Robert Brideport by order of the mayor		5d
Wax bought for sealing a certain warrant made to John Bosoun to be attorney of the mayor and community at the common bench		1d
Expenses of Roger atte Wille and Thomas Forsdone towards *Pratteshyde* to seize a ship for the earl of Lancaster		23d
Paid for the inventory of John Solas'		3d
Three men hired to guard the houses and goods of John Meattere for two nights and for candles		7d
To John de Chevereston for his labour going to Lostwithiel to carry there £10 of the prince's rent	6s	8d
One pair of boots given to Elias Wilde for his labour towards Chudleigh for common business		42d
Wine and fire bought on the day of the election of the mayor according to the custom of the city	3s	9d
Wine sent to the old mayor and the new, the old seneschals and the new, and the other officers the same day according to ancient custom	12s	
Total	74s	7d

Rent allowed

Seeks allowance of 18s 4d to the queen of England from his own cash	18s	4d[12]
For the tenement of William Harewill within the West Gate	4s	
For the tenement which William Vyke held in *Maudelynestrete* because it cannot be levied		20d
For the tenement of John Houpere within the North Gate next to the wall		12d
For the tenement which Gilbert Harpour held there		12d[13]
For three doors outside the East Gate next to *Hangemannesplace*		12d
For the tenement of Michael de Exstone next to the East Gate		12d
For a certain plot of John Eysy opposite All Hallows Goldsmith Street late of Sir Thomas Chageforde		6d[14]
For a certain lane there blocked up called . . . *ope comitelane*	2s	
For a gate of the archdeacon of Cornwall	2s	
For a gate of the Friars Preachers through which there is a way to the city wall	2s	

---

[12] *38s 4d* crossed through
[13] *12d* crossed through
[14] *6d* crossed through

For two plots which William de Pontyngdone held because they lie near to the tenement of the archdeacon of Totnes		16d
For the exit in the back part of the tenement of the archdeacon of Totnes	2s	
For the tenement which John Rok' held in Goldsmith Street	10s	
For a plot which William Cogan held between the city walls		1d
For a certain shop which John Holl' held on the west side of the Guildhall		40d
For a certain plot which John Uphavene held next to the entry of his messuage		1d
For a plot of Master Walter Gyffard next to his porch		6d
For a tenement which Richard Gyffard held next to the North Gate	2s	8d
For the prior of Plympton for having and making a certain step in the king's highway before the tenement of the said prior next to the Bishop's Gate		4d
For one close on the front side of the tenement of John de Chuddelegh next to the Bishop's Gate		6d
For a certain beam [*trabe*] situated in the king's highway which William Dauney held		4d
For rent around the pillory because it was empty for the same time	7s	
Paid to Thomas Spicer by order of the mayor because the same Thomas at the foot of his account was short [*exc'*] by so great an amount	8s	10½d
For the fine of Alexander Leche because they [*sic*] cannot be levied	6s	8d
Allowed to Thomas Forsdon, Henry Stam' and John Chevereston bailiffs on their account for amercements which were condoned by the mayor and others which could not be levied for three quarters both for amercements of court and for the mayor's tourn as is shown by the account of the bailiffs	53s	1d
Allowance which was condoned to John Lurlegh for his estreats for various amercements condoned and other things which cannot be levied as is shown by a certain schedule annexed to this account	69s	3d
Condoned for various amercements of the bakers of the arrears of the account of John White	7s	
Condoned to John Criditon'		8d
Condoned to John Somaistre, dyer [*deghere*] for his rent because a wall fell on his house	6s	8d
Total £10	11s	4½d

Sum total of all payments expended and allowed
   deducted from the total of the charge above and
   he owes £7 13s 2½d. Of which 10s is allowed to
   him as an aid to his fee. And so he owes £7 3s
   2½d. And he finds a pledge to pay the aforesaid
   cash at the feast of St Peter ad Vincula next to
   come. But of the aforesaid sum he afterwards
   charges himself in another account with cash
   received for work on the bridge. And thus he is
   acquitted.   £78   19s   10½d

[Names of pledges:]

John Spic[er]	Robert de Bredeport	John Spicer
William Stockelegh	mayor	Roger atte Wille
Richard Oliver	Robert Nobel	William Benet[15]
Robert Broun	Robert Broun	
	William Wyke	
	Richard Oliver	

This account was paid on Tuesday after the feast of
   St Barnabas the Apostle 25 Edward III

Names of the auditors

Robert Broun	Roger atte Wille
Robert Noble	William Stockelegh
John Spicer	John Holl
Robert Broun	Richard Whithorn
William Wyke	
Richard Oliver	

Memorandum that the bailiffs' accounts were
   delivered to John Gyst to transcribe and return
   within eight days   £10   13s   0½d

1349–50 ACCOUNT OF JOHN SPYCER, SENESCHAL AND RECEIVER OF THE COMMON GOODS OF THE AFORESAID CITY, FROM MICHAELMAS 23 EDWARD III TO THE SAME FEAST IN THE FOLLOWING YEAR

Fixed rents
Rents of the said city both in the city and in the
   suburbs of the same city for a whole year with the
   rent of one messuage of *Pratteshide*   £6   14s   1d
Rent of the farm of Duryard   £32
Passage of *Prattishide* nothing because the boat is
   completely broken but will be repaired in the
   future

                                        Total   £38   14s   1d

[15]*William Benet* crossed through

Issues of the city

Custom of fish	£7	6s	8d
Custom of meat		33s	4d
Petty customs		20s	
Custom of bread		4s	
Custom of flour		5s	6d
Custom of oil			5d
Grazing sold between the North Gate and *Wyndesore*			18d[1]
Grazing sold at *Crolledych* [Southernhay]			12d
St Nicholas' Fair		29s	
Issues of the pyx for the whole year		35s	8d
Custom of wine for the same time		52s[2]	
Custom of iron and other merchandise for the same time		33s	7d
Custom of woad		2s	
Nothing from the passage[3] because it is above			
Stallage when meat was sold		2s	
Total	£18	6s	8d
Fines of workmen [*operariorum*]		52s	1d
Total		52s	1d

Profits of courts

Amercements of the courts for the whole year as is shown by the estreats of the bailiffs	£8	7s	2d[4]
Amercements of the mayor's tourns the same year		70s	9d[5]
Amercements of the examination of the measures the same year		16s	3d[6]
Entrants to the freedom the same year	£8		8d
For fines and various redemptions etc. the same year as is shown by the rolls of the courts		59s[7]	
For waif cattle forfeited and strays the same year as is shown by the rolls of the courts		55s	6½d[8]
Amercements of the bakers for the whole year		22s	10½d[9]
From the executors of Hamo de Dyreworthy for damage done in Duryard Wood as accounted for by inquisition		40s	
For bagavel and burgavel the same year		40s	
Total	£31	12s	5d
Sum Total of the whole charge	£91	5s	3d

[1] *18d* underlined
[2] *53s 3d* crossed through
[3] *Nothing from the passage* crossed through
[4] *10s 4d* crossed through
[5] *61s 9d* crossed through
[6] *6d* crossed through
[7] *56s 2d* crossed through
[8] *47s 6½d* crossed through
[9] *13s 8d* crossed through

Rents paid

To John Kendale receiver of lord Edward price of Wales and duke of Cornwall for the rent of the farm of the aforesaid city for Easter and Michaelmas terms as is shown by three quittances	£20		
To the clerk of the said John Kendale for having quittance		4s	
To the prior of Holy Trinity London for the rent of the aforesaid city for Easter and Michaelmas terms as is shown by two quittances	£25	12s	6d
To the parish chaplains of the aforesaid city for the two terms of the year according to custom		4s	8d
Total	£46		14d

Fees paid

To Robert Brydeport mayor of the aforesaid city for his fee for the whole year	100s	
To the three seneschals for their fees for the same time	60s	
To John Spycer bailiff and receiver	40s	
To William Wyke for the same time	40s	
To Martin the clerk for his fee	40s	
To the four keepers of the gates of the aforesaid city for the same time	12s	
To Robert Brydeport attorney in the lord king's bench as is shown by quittance	20s	
To John Bosoun attorney in the common bench[10]	13s	4d
To Nicholas Whytying'	20s[11]	
To Robert atte Weye for his fee	20s[12]	
To the four bailiffs for their fees for the whole year	40s	4d
For robes of the said bailiffs for Christmas	44s	
For bread and wine sent to the mayor and other officers for Christmas according to the custom of the city	17s	9½d[13]
For bread and wine sent to the mayor, seneschals and other offices for Easter	19s	1d[14]
Total	£25	6s	6d

Gifts and presents

One gallon of wine sent to the mayor on his arrival before he received his office		12d
Sent to Sir William de Schareshulle on his first arrival at the assize held in Lent four gallons of wine price	2s	8d

[10]*Rec; non habet acquiet'* written above
[11]*H diem ad redd' acquiet' cum arrer'* in margin; *Rec' habet acquiet'* written above
[12]*non habet acquiet'* written above
[13]*14s 9d* crossed through
[14]*16s 11½d* crossed through

To Richard Bortone at the same time two gallons of wine		16d
To the said Sir William at another time at the same assizes four gallons of wine	2s	8d
To Richard Borton at the same time two gallons of wine		16d
To James Husoe one gallon of wine		8d
To William Fyffide one gallon of wine		8d
To Edmund Chelry one gallon of wine		8d
To John de Schareshull precentor and Sir Adam de Schareshull two gallons of wine		16d
To Robert Elleford the lord prince's esquire two gallons of wine		16d
Sent to the bishop of Exeter six gallons of wine	4s	6d
To a certain messenger of the lord king called Fox carrying a writ to exonerate all ships within the port [*portagium*] 50 barrels		12d
To the prince's bailiff for having respite of rent from Easter to the arrival of John Daubernoun		12d
To John Daubernoun's clerk for carrying 100s towards Lostwithiel		12d
Sent to John Dyneham knight, John Ralegh, John Loterel, Richard de Brankescomb, William de Aumarle and Roger Pyperel justices of oyer and terminer etc. on two occasions, seven and a half gallons of wine	5s	
To Hugh de Aftone two gallons of wine		16d
To John Fyfide, Edmund Chelry and Peter Chard three gallons of wine	2s	
To Richard Bortone two gallons of wine		16d
To John Kendale and Thomas Havener two gallons of wine		16d
Total	32s	2d

Necessary expenses

For cleaning the conduit in Coombe Street for the safety of the city walls	2s	
For mats bought for benches in the Guildhall of Exeter		7d
For making 12 boards for placing the fish on and selling and 24 trestles and for buying the boards and timber for the trestles and for nails and one cask bought for the boards	12s	2d
For parchment and ink bought for the whole year *viz* for the court roll and other necessary things etc.	7s	
To his clerk writing and entering an account and other business done at the same time	10s	

For cleaning the conduit at Coombe Street for the safety of the walls		14d
For cleaning the Guildhall of Exeter for St Nicholas' fair		2d
To the parson of the church of St Pancras for the tenth of St Nicholas' fair	2s	
To the boy carrying the table for placing fish on and for selling it for the whole year	2s	
For mending and repairing the forms [*formular*'] in the Guildhall and for tables and nails bought for the same		12d
For maintenance for the horses of Master Thomas Lyncolne *leche* forfeited		6d
For one wall made between Richard Whythorn and the Guildhall		7d
For fire bought on election day of the mayor and seneschals		8d
For wine bought on the same day	2s	
For 15 gallons of wine sent to the mayor, new officers and old officers the same day	10s	
Total	51s	10d

Foreign expenses

For the expenses of Roger atte Wille and Martin Batteshull clerk going to Sherborne after Robert Brideport's election to the mayoralty by order of the community for five days' allowance	7s	8d
For the hire of horses of the said Roger and Martin for the same time	2s	6d
For one and a half gallons of wine given to the taxers of the tenth part of the city of Exeter		12d
For one gallon of wine given to the men being at the mayor's tourn		8d
Wine given to the taxers of the mayor's tourn		4d
Given to the taxers of the amercements of the city court between Michaelmas and Christmas		4d
For maintenance of various cattle [*averiorum*] coming as strays at various times		12d
To the buyers of customs of fish, meat etc. for Christmas		8d
To Gilbert son of Oliver de Wybbery of the last wool [*ultimis lanis*]	20s	
For the expenses of various jurors being at Exeter the Saturday before Palm Sunday before William de Schareshull for hearing and determining a certain trespass at the suit of William de Welham	5s	6d
For wine given to the buyers of customs for Easter		8d
To a certain messenger of the lord king by order of the mayor		6d

To a certain messenger carrying letters to London of Robert de Brideport attorney in the king's bench for having exoneration for ten men at arms	6s	8d
	[½ mark]	
Delivered to William Wyke towards London for the purchase of a writ of the lord king for allowing a charter	6s	8d
	[½ mark]	
To workmen for making the city wall adjoining the East Gate		12d
For the expenses of the mayor, receiver and other citizens going to *Colepole* to seize a certain ship for the prince's suit		10d
To the reeve of Topsham for two salmon seized in Lent by order of the mayor	13s	4d
For the expenses of one bailiff sent to Dartmouth for two days and one night		12d
Given to the buyers of customs for the feast of the Nativity of St John the Baptist one gallon of wine		8d
To the reeve of Topsham for one third of the custom of wine	17s	9¼d
Given to one boy going after Nicholas Whytynge being against William Welham for the arrival of Sir William de Schareshull from Cornwall		6d
For the expenses of the said Nicholas for four days	4s	
To Thomas Bolset the lord king's messenger by order of the mayor	2s	
To the buyers of customs for Michaelmas one gallon of wine		8d
To a certain messenger called Cardinal		6d
For two locks bought for the cellar doors and others		6d
Total £4	16s	11¼d

Rent deficits

The tenement of William Harewille within the West Gate	4s	
Vyke Tenement in *Maudelynestrete*		20d
[The tenement of] John Houpere within the North Gate next to the wall		12d
Three doors outside the East Gate next to *Hangemanesplace*		12d
The tenth of the rent of the house of *Pratteshyde*	2s	2d
The tenement of Michael de Exston next to the East Gate		12d
The gate of the archdeacon of Cornwall	2s	
The gate of the Friars Preachers through which there is a way to the city wall	2s	

Two plots which William de Pontingdone held next to the tenement of the archdeacon of Totnes		16d
The exit in the back part of the tenement of the archdeacon of Totnes	2s	
A certain plot above the North Gate which the rector of the church of St Paul holds		6d
The tenement of a certain John Rok' in Goldsmith Street	10s	
A tenement which William Cogan held between the city walls		1d
A shop next to the Guildhall on the west side because it was empty for three terms	7s	
A certain plot which John de Uphavene held		1d
A plot of Walter Gyffard next to the North Gate		6d
The tenement which John Dollyng sometime held next to the South Gate	3s	
The tenement which Richard Gyffard held next to the North Gate	2s	8d
The prior of Plympton for having a certain . . . [*word omitted*] next to the king's street in front of the tenement of the said prior		4d
A certain plot which John Dollyng sometime held outside the South Gate behind his tenement		12d
For one close in front of the tenement of John de Chuddelegh next to the Bishop's Gate		6d
A certain beam [*trab'*] situated in the king's street which William Dauney marshal held		4d
A rent about the pillory which is vacant	6s	4d
The tenement of Gilbert Harpour'		12d
Total	51s	6d

[*Dorse*]

Allowances

William Caubyn and William Bavy who were amerced for trespass made against the peace of which 40s was condoned by the mayor at the instance of the Friars Preachers	3s	4d
Of the amercement of John Caulesweye baker because he withdrew from the town before the receipt of the estreats[15]	11s	8d[16]
Various amercements condoned by the mayor and other seneschals and of the amercements held of the tenants of St Nicholas and St Stephen, as is shown by the account of Henry Stam, William Bruwere, John Cheverestone bailiffs	15s	5d

[15]*and amercements condoned* [*to the other bakers* crossed through] written above
[16]*3s 4d* crossed through

Various amercements in the mayor's tourn and the amercements of measures condoned by the mayor and the amercements held of the tenants of the fees of St Nicholas and St Stephen and others who withdrew from the town before the receipt of the extreats as is shown in the account of the said bailiffs · 15s 9d

Amercements condoned by the mayor and other bailiffs, amercements which cannot be levied and amercements held of the tenants of the fees of St Nicholas and St Stephen as is shown in the account of John Lurlegh · 11s 3d

Amercements of the mayor's tourn which cannot be levied and amercements condoned and of the fees of St Nicholas and St Stephen as is shown by the account of the said John because it was accounted for late · 3s 9d

Work of the bailiffs for collecting fines and amercements of workmen · 2s 6d[17]

Total	57s	10d
Sum total of all expenses and allowances £85	17s	11¼d
which deducted from the above charge he owes	107s	4¾d

Of which they allow to the same 40d of the fine of John Cokelescomb which cannot be levied, 20d of the fine of Richard Mounteyn, 18d of the fine of William Chevereston, 4d of the fine of John Screcche, 6s 9d of the fines of workmen which cannot be levied, 11d of the fine of Walter Leche, and 40d condoned to John Somaister dyer of his rent. And the sum of the allowances is 17s 10d. And thus he owes £4 9s 5¾d net. And 9s is condoned to the same which he says he spent on the justices in the absence of the mayor and other bailiffs. And he pays 10s 5d on account. And thus he owes 70s 0¼d. And thus finds pledges to pay on the feast of the Purification of the Blessed Virgin Mary next coming, *viz* Thomas Spicer, Robert Broun, Roger atte Wille, William Stockelegh and Roger Haycombe. And there it is paid to William Wyke for the common business going to London. To Alexander Oldeston with other cash for the work of the bridge 31s 2d. And allowed to him 3s 4d which Richard Ellewill and 6d of William Torpelegh condoned. And he owes 15s 0¼d which the assigns of Alexander Oldeston paid in part of his debt. And thus he is quit.

[17]entry crossed through

Names of the auditors

Robert Nobel	John Swaneton
Thomas Spicer	Richard Somaistre
John Gyst	Roger atte Wille
Robert Broun	Alexander Oldeston
John Somaister	William Stockelegh
Robert Hugheton	John Brounewill

The account of rents the Wednesday in the feast of St Thomas the Apostle the 25th year of the reign of King Edward the third.

Memorandum that the said 10s 5½d is in the custody of the mayor in the chest in the provostry with the cash of the lord king's collection.

1350–1 ACCOUNT OF ROBERT BROWN, SENESCHAL AND RECEIVER OF THE COMMON GOODS OF THE CITY AFORESAID, FROM MICHAELMAS 24 EDWARD III TO THE SAME DATE IN THE FOLLOWING YEAR

Fixed rents

Rent of the city and the suburbs for a whole year with the rent of *Pratteshyde*	£6	14s	1d
Farm of Duryard this year	£32		
Nothing from the passage at *Pratisshide* because there is no boat there			
Total	£38	14s	1d

Issues of the city

Custom of fish this year	£8	6s	8d
Custom of meat		36s	8d
Petty customs		33s	4d
Custom of flour		6s	8d
Issues of the pyx for the whole year		32s	1d
Grazing sold this year		5s	6d
Custom of wine		71s	
Custom of iron and other merchandise as is shown by the court rolls		20s	6d
Custom of woad			12d
From St Nicholas' fair		43s	
Timber sold coming from a house formerly of Nicholas Rok' in Goldsmith Street		5s	
Custom of bread		5s	
Custom of oil			12d
Received from the sale of stalls when meat was sold as is shown by the court roll		18s	8d[1]
Total	£22	6s	1d

[1] *15s* crossed through

Profits of the courts

Various amercements this year as is shown by	£12		
the estreats of the bailiffs			11d
From the mayor's tourn this year	£6	3s	3d
From entrants into the freedom		33s	4d
From various fines and redemptions as is shown etc		50s	4d
From the amercements of the bakers[2]		39s	8d
From waif and stray cattle		5s	6d
From bagavel and burgavel this year as is shown by the court roll		42s	
Total	£26	15s	
Total of the whole charge	£87	15s	2d

Rents paid

To John Kendale receiver of lord Edward prince of Wales and duke of Cornwall for the rent of the farm of the city aforesaid for Easter term and Michaelmas	£20		
To the clerk of the said John to have a quittance		4s	
To the prior of Holy Trinity London for the rent of the city aforesaid for Easter and Michaelmas terms as is shown by two quittances	£25	12s	6d
Paid to the parish chaplains of the city aforesaid at the two terms of the year by custom		4s	8d
Total	£46		14d

Fees paid to the mayor and other officers

To Robert Brydeport mayor of the city aforesaid for his fee for the year		100s	
To the three seneschals for the same time		60s	
To Robert Broun the receiver for the same time		40s	
To William Wyke		60s	
To Martin the clerk for the same time		33s	4d
To the three bailiffs for the whole year		30s	3d
For the robes of the four bailiffs		44s	6d
For the shearing of the said cloth			12d[3]
To the four keepers of the gates of the city aforesaid for the whole year		12s	
Bread and wine sent to the mayor, seneschals other officers for Christmas according to the custom of the city		16s	5d[4]
Bread and wine sent to the mayor, seneschals etc. for Easter		19s	1d[5]
To John Chope for half the year		13s	4d
Total	£21	9s	11d

[2] *and amercements of false weight* above line
[3] *18d* crossed through
[4] *21s 7d* crossed through
[5] *21s 7d* crossed through

Foreign fees paid[6]

To Nicholas Whytyng for his pension this year	20s	
To Robert atte Weye	20s	
To Robert de Brideport attorney of the community at the lord king's bench	20s	
To John Bosoun attorney at the common bench	13s	4d
Total	73s	4d

Necessary Expenses

Parchment bought and ink for the court roll of the mayor's tourn and other business done throughout the whole year	6s	8d
For his clerk writing and entering his account for the same time	10s	
Lime [*calice*][7] bought for the hall of the Guildhall & covering the solar	2s	
Sand bought for the same		3d
Mats bought for the hall		7d
Mending one lock for the cellar under the hall		1d
Mending and cleaning of the conduit next to *Crikelepitte*	3s	8d
Men hired to carry timber and stones taken in the name of distraint at the corner next to the house of Robert Clyne at the Guildhall	2s	1d
Two roofers with his [sic] boys to roof the Guildhall and the chamber hire etc.	3s	11½d
Nails and wedges bought for the same		4d
Timber and tables bought to mend the pillory	14s	
Carpentry and sawing of the said timber	16s	
Nails and staples bought for the same	4s	
Resin, pitch and tallow bought for the same		12d
Lead bought to put round the wood of the pillory	2s	8d
Mending the pipe next to the quarry outside the East Gate and solder bought for the same		16d
Wax bought for the indictment		2d
Timber bought for the bridge of the East Gate from Richard atte Forde and for making and sawing of the said timber	15s	4d
One beam bought to carry the said bridge		18d
Carriage of the aforesaid timber	2s	
Nuncheon for the workers on various occasions		10d
One beam bought to make one *walplate* and one small log to put above the bridge[8]	2s	
For packing [*paccam'*]		3d

[6]*he has no quittance but . . . to . . . in margin below heading
[7]perhaps cup
[8]*carriage of the said timber 12d* crossed through

A boy hired to clean the hall and chamber for the feasts of St Nicholas, Christmas and St John the Baptist			6d
Rushes bought for the same			6d
Cleaning the chest under the pillory			1d
New locks bought and old ones mended with keys for the same about the pillory			12d
Mending three locks and three keys bought for the coffer in the solar			10d
Wax bought to seal a letter sent to Bordeaux			1d
Buying two locks and two keys for the chapel over the East Gate			6d
Mending the benches in the solar			4d
Carrying roofing stones from the Guildhall to the East Gate			6d
One seam of straw bought to put in the Guildhall			5d
A lock bought to keep the prisoners under the pillory			4d
Two men hired with two horses for three[9] days' allowance etc. and a half		2s	4d
	Total	£4 18s	1½d

Foreign payments

To Nicholas Wytyng' and Robert Bymystr' for their expenses at parliament held at Westminster by order of the mayor		60s[10]	
To Richard Ellewille to have a transcript of the new statute		3s	4d
To the parson of the church of St Pancras for the tenth of St Nicholas' fair		2s	
To the provost of Topsham for the custom of wine belonging to the lord earl for the third part		23s	8d
	Total	£4 9s	

Gifts and presents

Cretan wine and bread sent to the lord bishop of Exeter		3s	4d
To the taxers of amercements of the courts on various occasions			8d
Wine sent to Richard de Bortone[11] and Richard Brankescombe at the assizes in Lent before their crossing to Cornwall and after to hear and determine on occasions 13 gallons price		8s	8d
Wine[12] given to buyers of the customs for Christmas			8d

[9]*two* crossed through
[10]*£4* crossed through
[11]*John de Stouford* crossed through
[12]written above line

Sent to a certain serjeant at arms of the lord king
lieutenant of Thomas Cok' knight one gallon of
wine price   8d
Sent to Walter de Harewill and his colleague
serjeants at arms of the lord king arriving to seize
ships one gallon of wine   8d
To the buyers of customs for Easter one gallon of
wine   8d
Wine sent to Richard Bortone[13] on two occasions
four gallons of wine price   2s   8d
Four gallons of wine sent to Philip de Wytton and
Walter Harewill being at the house of John Sleghe   2s   6d[14]
Wine sent to Robert Hacche sheriff of Devon   16d
To the buyers of customs for the feast of the Nativity
of St John one gallon of wine   8d
Wine sent to Edmund Chelrey and Henry Grene   16d
Two gallons of Cretan wine sent to the mayor by
Henry Stam[15]   2s   8d
Wine sent to Richard Borton[16] and the other justices
in the autumn six gallons of wine   4s
Wine sent to Edmund Chelrey one trenchard two
gallons[17]
Fire given and two gallons of wine in the Guildhall
on the day of the election of the mayor,
seneschals and other officers according to the
custom of the city   2s   4d
Wine sent to the mayor the same day two gallons   16d[18]
To John Spicer one gallon   8d[18]
To the buyers of the customs for Michaelmas one
gallon of wine   8d
15 gallons of wine sent to the mayor, seneschals and
other officers on election day according to the
custom of the city   10s

                                                        Total   41s

Foreign expenses
Two bailiffs sent to *Pratteshyde* to seize ships and
sailors by order of Walter Harewill for one day
and one night and for hire of horses   16d
William Bruwere the bailiff sent to *Chexstone* for
seizing men by order of the aforesaid Walter   3d
Martin Batteshull going to *Colepole* on business for
John de Wyttone and Walter de Harewill and
with hire of one horse   9d

[13] *John Stouford* crossed through
[14] Entry crossed through
[15] *as a present* above line
[16] *John de Stouford* crossed through
[17] *price 16d* crossed through
[18] entry crossed through

William Borne going to *Pratteshid* on two occasions to seize ships		12d
One horse hired for Martin the clerk going to *Colecomb* with the mayor to receive the statute concerning the lord earl for two days		6d
Bread for the aforesaid horse		2d
Carriage of one pipe of wine to the earl to Exminster and back to Exeter	2s	
For loading & unloading the aforesaid pipe in a wagon		4d
? Brass [*eru*] for the said pipe		1d
John Lurleigh towards Lostwithiel to take £10 to the receiver of the lord prince	3s	4d
Total	9s	9d

Rent deficits

The tenement of William de Harewill within the West Gate	4s	
The Vyke tenement in *Maudelynestre*		20d
The tenement of John Houpere within the East Gate		12d
The tenement of Gilbert Harpour next to the North Gate		12d
Three doors next to *Hangemannesplace* outside the East Gate		12d
Decrease in rent for the house at *Pratteshyde*	2s	2d
The tenement of Michael Exstone next to the East Gate		12d
The gate of the archdeacon of Cornwall	2s	
The gate of the Friars Preachers through which there is a way to the city walls[19]		
The gate which was William Bykelegh's now in the hands of the Friars Preachers		6d
Two plots which William Pontyngdone held which lie near to the tenement of the archdeacon of Totnes		16d
The exit in the back part of the tenement of the archdeacon of Totnes	2s	
A certain plot above the North Gate which the rector of the church of St Paul held		6d
The tenement which John Rok' held in Goldsmith Street	10s	
A plot which William Cogan held between the walls of the city		1d
The shop which John Screcche held next to the Guildhall because it has been empty for three terms	7s	

[19] *2s crossed through*

A certain plot which John Uphavene held next to
   the entrance of his messuage   1d
A plot of Master Walter Gyffard next to his porch   6d
The tenement of John Dolling next to the South
   Gate   3s
The tenement of Richard Gyffard next to the North
   Gate   2s   8d
The prior of Plympton for making and having a
   certain step in the king's highway next to the
   Bishop's Gate   4d
A plot which John Dolling held next to his tenement   12d
A certain beam situated in the king's highway
   which William Dauney held   4d
The rent about the pillory because it is empty   6s
The tenement of John Brideport next to *La*
   Flexfold [20]

	Total	49s	2d[21]

Chope's allowance

Seeks allowance of 27s[22] for amercements condoned
   by the mayor and seneschals in the fees of St
   Nicholas and St Stephen as is shown by the
   account of John Chope to the underbailiffs *viz*   27s

condoned by the mayor and community

Walter Crisp *leche*	3s	4d
Roger Nyenwetone		3d
Adam Manelegh		3d
Richard Braylegh	3s	4d
John Somaystre *deghere*		2d
Henry Forb[our] and Thomas Ferbour		9d
Thomas Ferbour		3d
Thomas Kyngeston'		3d
Richard Dygoun		3d
Roger Pestour		18d

in the fee of St Stephen

Richard Plomere	[23]
Matilda Obelyn	2d
Richard Segere	[24]

[20] *18d* crossed through
[21] *51s 2d* crossed through
[22] *29s* crossed through
[23] *3d* crossed through
[24] *4d* crossed through

in the fee of St Nicholas

Gilbert Muleward		2d
Stephen Crokkernewill		25

in the fee of Exeter Castle

William Caubyn	3s	4d
Elias Whyet		3d

received from the town

Thomas Hale		3d
John Reymound		3d
Richard servant to Richard Chuseldene		3d
Richard Forbour	3s	4d
Henry Pelyter of London	2s	6d
John Chevereston'		2d
William Cheverestone		3d
Richard Forbour		2d
William Obelyn		2d
Richard Peyntour		4d
John Conere		3d
Reginald Trenans		2d
John son of John Marsshal	2s	6d

by John Gyst

William Monioun[26]		
Baldwin Polgrun and Is' his wife	2s	6d

by R Broun

Richard Goldsmith		3d
John Chope		2d
Adam Bedman because he is poor		1d

[*Dorse*]

Bruwere's allowance

Seeks allowance of 16s for amercements condoned
by the mayor and other officers in the fees of
St Nicholas and St Stephen as is shown in the
account of William Bruwere *viz*   16s

[25] *1d* crossed through
[26] entry crossed through

condoned by the mayor and community

Richard Goldsmith		3d
Matthew Barbour		3d
Thomas Forbour		18d
Adam King' baker	2s	6d
Matthew Barbour		1d
Gilbert Muleward		4d
Stephen Bollok'		2d
Nicholas son of Nicholas de Halb'	2s	6d
William Caperoun chaplain		15d
bailiffs because they did not distrain Alice Coterel		12d
Stephen Bollok'		2d
Roger Pestour	2s	6d

received from the town

John Chevereston' and William Halbton' baker	2s	6d
Philip Byryman		3d
the same Philip		4d

St Nicholas

William Kerdewill'	2d

St Stephen

Joan Pyn	3d

Large's allowance

Seeks alllowance of 3s 9d condoned by the mayor
and other officers and in the fees of St Nicholas
and St Stephen as is shown by the account of

John Large *viz*	3s	9d

condoned by the mayor

Nicholas son of Nicholas de Halb'	2s	6d
Mathew Barbour		2d

received from the town

William Cheverestone	1d
Philip Buryman	2d
Juliana Onger	1d
Richard Fot	2d
Thomas Dauney	1d
John Speare	2d

because he is poor

Thomas Russel	1d

condoned by R Broun

    Nicholas Parchmenere   1d

condoned by J Gyst

    Richard Frauncesbe'   2d

in the fee of St Nicholas

    John Sherman   2d

Stam's allowance

Seeks allowance of 15s 9d[27] for amercements
    condoned by the mayor and other officers and in
    the fees of St Nicholas and St Stephen as is shown
    by the account of Henry Stam *viz*   15s   9d

condoned by the mayor

Margery Cole	40d
Hugh Ferbour	40d
Joan Huxham	40d[28]
Matthew Barbour	3d
Clarice Plente	40d

received from the town

    Richard Bovy   2d

in the fee of St Nicholas

John Scherman	2d
Robert Wolbeatere	3d[29]

condoned by Thomas Spicer

John Screeche	4d
Adam atte Wode	3d
Nicholas atte Comb'	2d

received from the town

Is' Durham	3d
Roger Orlager	6d

condoned by R Broun

bailiffs	4d
Christine Deghere	2d

[27]*7s 10d* crossed through
[28]*20d* crossed through
[29]entry crossed through

Stam's allowance
Seeks to allow himself 3s 3d[30] for amercements in
the mayor's tourn condoned by the mayor and
other officers and in the fees of St Nicholas and St
Stephen as is shown in the account of Henry
Stam *viz*   3s   3d

condoned by the mayor

John Conce	3d
Adam Brasyutere	3d
Adam Kyng' baker	8d
Richard Portesham	3d
John atte Mille[31]	4d

received from the town

John Spycer	3d
Richard Samforde	6d

in the fee of St Stephen

Is' Synegere	3d
Matilda Obelyn	3d
Emma Pottere	3d[32]

in the fee of St Nicholas

Amicia wife of Stephen Crokk'	3d[33]
Richard Houpere	3d[34]

by R Broun

Joan wife of Walter atte Wode	3d

Borne's allowance
Seeks allowance of 9s 9d for amercements condoned
in the mayor's tourn by the mayor and other
officers and in the fees of St Nicholas and
St Stephen as is shown in the account of William
Borne *viz*   9s   9d

condoned by the mayor

Richard Bradecroft'	12d
Thomas Founteyn	4d
Emma Tappestere	3d
Gilbert Doune	3d

[30] *4s* crossed through
[31] *because in the tourn* above line
[32] entry crossed through
[33] *3d* crossed through
[34] *3d* crossed through

Sarah Stole	4d
Matilda Torylox	2d
Gylda Waryn	3d
John Hostilere	6d
William Lylox	3d
Is' atte Wille	3d

received from the town

Julian Spycer	3d
Alice Tappestere	2d

in the fee of St Nicholas

Walter Spek'	6d
the same Walter	6d

outside the West Gate

Walter Stenehalle	12d
Ralph Berlegh'	12d
Thomas atte More	12d
William Rondel	6d
John Gynys	3d
John Beyvyn	6d
Richard Beyvyn	6d

Bruwere's allowance
Seeks allowance of 6s 6d for amercements condoned
   in the mayor's tourn by the mayor and other
   officers and in the fees of St Nicholas and St
   Stephen as is shown by the account of William
   Bruwere *viz*   6s   6d

condoned by the mayor

Helewisa Noble		6d
Is' Gyst		4d
Joan Olyver		4d
Agatha Spycer		3d
Emma Hughetone		3d
Gilbert Saghiere		10d
Alice Chamberlayn		3d
Richard Braylegh'	2s	

in the fee of St Nicholas

Walter Bayg'	6d
Luke Hobbe	3d
Walter Bayg'	3d
John Rof'	3d
Christine Clyne	3d

because in the tourn

    Roger Mol'   3d

Large's allowance
Seeks allowance of 4s 9d[35] for amercements in the
mayor's tourn by the mayor and other officers
and in the fees of St Nicholas and St Stephen as
by the account of John Large *viz*   4s   9d

condoned by the mayor

John Haye	3d
Thomas Bakere	2d
John Brounewill' junior	3d
Ralph Bakere	3d
Richard Dych'	3d
Elena Gyst'	3d

in the fee of St Stephen

Henry Barbour	6d
Clarice Spirlake	3d
Edith Obelyn	3d
and John Sleghe	7d

received from the tourn

Alice Swilledone	3d
Denis Brente	3d
Thomas Hale	3d
Alice atte Hole	3d
John Noreys	3d

by Thomas Spycer

John Chope	3d
Robert Corteys	3d

Seeks allowance of 12s 5d[36] of amercements of the
bakers and false measures condoned by the
mayor and also amercements which cannot be
levied   12s   5d

which cannot be levied

John Frere	40d
the same John	6d
Hugh Conaunt	6d
John Frere	6d
John Frere	6d

[35] *2d* crossed through
[36] *11d* crossed through

the same John	3d
John Frere	9d
Hugh Conaunt	6d

condoned by the mayor.

Laur' Botour	12d
Richard Walsch	12d
Richard Gyst	3d
Stephen Bollok'	6d
Richard Grybbe	6d
the same Richard[37]	6d
Walter Bakere	4d

Robert Polleworthy because in the pillory		2s	
Total of allowances	£4	19s	4d
Total of expenses and allowances	£90	10s	9½d

And thus the total of the charge exceeds the total of the discharge by   55s   7½d[38]

. . . memorandum that the Friars Preachers paid 6s for their rent for their gate for three years and are in the keeping of the mayor with the other cash.

[*At foot of account:*] Exeter rolls of various accounts of the receivers of the common goods of the city aforesaid

1351–2 THE ACCOUNT OF JOHN SWANETON, SENESCHAL AND RECEIVER OF THE COMMON GOODS OF THE AFORESAID CITY, FROM MICHAELMAS 25 EDWARD III TO THE SAME DATE 26 [EDWARD III]

Fixed rents

Rents of the city and suburbs with the rent of *Pratteshyde* for the whole year	£6	14s	1d
Rent of the farm of Duryard	£32		
Increase in rent for a certain lane next to the church of St Kerrian			6d
Increase of rent for the shop which William Rondel holds at *Fysfolde* for a half year			18d
For the passage nothing this year because there is no boat			
Increase of rent for three beams in the High Street			12d
Total	£38	17s	1d

[37] *John* crossed through
[38] *He has a Memorandum to repeat the account for various reasons And not allowed by the final account* in margin

Issues of the city

Custom of fish this year	£8	6s	8d
Custom of meat		30s	
Petty customs sold		33s	4d
Custom of flour sold		6s	8d
Custom of woad			18d
Issues of St Nicholas' Fair this year		40s	
Issues of the pyx for the whole year		15s	1d
Grazing sold this year		3s	5d
Custom of oil			18d
Custom of wine		48s	3d
Custom of iron and other merchandise as is shown by the court rolls		21s	0½d[1]
Custom of bread sold		2s	6d
For stalls where meat is sold		20s	2d
Total	£19	10s	1½d

Profits of the courts

Various amercements of the courts this year as is shown by the bailiffs' estreats	£30	3s	11¾d
From the mayor's tourn	£4	15s	4d
From entrants into the freedom this year		39s	4d
Cattle of felons and waifs		9s	5d
Amercements of the bakers		27s	1d
Bagavel and burgavel		36s	8d
Amercements of false measures		13s	1d
Waif cattle			8d
Total	£41	5s	6¾d
Total of the whole change	£99	12s	9¼d

Rent deficits

The tenement of William Harewille within the West Gate		4s
Vyke tenement in *Maudelynestre*		20d
The tenement of John Houpere within the East Gate		12d
The tenement of Gilbert Harpourt next to the North Gate		12d
Three [?doors] outside the East Gate next to *Hangemanseplace*		12d
Decrease in rent for the tenement of *Prattishide*	2s	2d
The gate of the archdeacon of Cornwall	2s	
The gate of Friars Preachers through which there is a way to the city walls	2s	
The gate formerly of William Bykelegh now in the hands of the Friars Preachers		6d

[1] *1d* crossed through

Two plots which William de Pontyngdone held which lie near to the tenement of the archdeacon of Totnes		16d
The exit at the back of the tenement of the archdeacon of Totnes	2s	
A certain plot above the North Gate		6d
The tenement formerly of John Rok' in Goldsmith Street	10s	
The plot which William Cogan held between the city walls		1d
The shop which John Screcche held next to the Guildhall	6s	
A certain plot which John Uphavene held next to the entrance of his messuage		1d
The plot of Master Walter Gyffard next to his porch		6d
The tenement of John Dollyng next to the South Gate	3s	
From the prior of Plympton for making a certain step in the king's highway next to the Bishop's Gate		4d
The plot which John Dollyng' held next to his tenement		12d
A certain beam situated in the king's highway which William Dauney held		4d
Rents around the pillory because they are empty for the whole year except one shop for one quarter and a half	7s	3d
Total	47s	9d

Rents paid

To the receiver of the cash of the lord prince of Wales and duke of Cornwall for the rent of the farm of the city aforesaid for Easter term as is shown by the quittance	£10		
To his clerk to have the quittance		2s	
To the prior of Holy Trinity London for the rent of the city aforesaid for Easter term as is shown by the quittance	£12	16s	3d
To the parish chaplains of the city aforesaid at the two terms of the year according to custom		4s	8d
Total	£23	2s	11d

Fees paid

To Robert de Brideport mayor of the city aforesaid for his fee for the whole year	100s
To the three seneschals	60s
To the receiver for the same time	40s
To William Wyke for the same time	60s
To Martin the clerk	40s

To the four bailiffs for their fees for the whole year		40s	4d
Four robes for the said bailiffs		46s	
Shearing of the aforesaid cloth			11d
To the four keepers of the gates of the aforesaid city for their fees for the whole year		12s	
For bread and wine sent to the mayor, seneschals and other officers for Christmas		19s	9d
Bread and wine sent to the mayor, seneschals and other officers for Easter according to the custom of the city aforesaid		21s	0½d
Four gallons of wine sent to the mayor at Michaelmas		2s	8d
To the receiver's clerk for making his account and other necessaries for the year		10s	
Wine on the day of the mayor's election one gallon			10d
Fires on the same day			9d
Total	£22	14s	3½d

Foreign payments

To Robert atte Weye for his fee for the year		20s	
To Nicholas Wytyng' for the same		20s	
To John Bosoun for the same		13s	4d
To Robert Brideport' attorney of the city at the lord king's bench		20s	
To Sir Hugh de Courtenay earl of Devon by order of the mayor		40s[2]	
The expenses of the mayor and others towards Northampton [*Northtone*] for the business of the community on Tuesday of the feast of St Petrock		21s	
To Simon atte Pytte and Thomas Spicere for their expenses to London at parliament for the community		40s	
To William Wyke for his expenses towards London for the business of the city by order of the mayor		20s	
One horse bought for the said William		17s	
To the rector of St Pancras for the tenth of St Nicholas' fair		2s	
To the sheriff of Devon for poundage of the goods [*pongag' averiorum*] of Thomas Kyngestone for green wax taken		7s	4d
The expenses of Thomas Spycer towards the earl of Devon to deliver the statute		2s	
To Richard Forestere for the third part of the custom of wine belonging to the lord earl		16s	1d
Total	£9	18s	9d

[2]entry crossed through

Gifts and presents

Wine sent to John Stonore and Richard Bortone justices of the lord king at the assizes next after the feast of the Conception of Blessed Mary four gallons of wine	2s	8d
Cretan wine sent to the same John and Richard at the same time		20d
One gallon of red wine and one gallon of white wine sent to Richard Bortone at the assize in Lent		18d
Wine sent to the aforesaid Richard and the other serjeants on another occasion in Lent two gallons of red wine		16d
One gallon of white wine		10d
Two gallons of wine sent to Hugh de Aftone in Lent		18d
One gallon of Cretan [wine] sent by Richard de Somaystre by order of the mayor		20d
One gallon of red wine		8d
Two gallons of red wine sent by John Spycere to Sir John Gray		16d
Bread sent to Peter de Gillesburgh	3s	8d
Wine sent to the same Peter by Thomas Spycere four gallons	2s	8d
White wine sent to the aforesaid Peter by the same Thomas	2s	
Wine sent to the same Peter by John Large one gallon		8d
One gallon of red wine sent to the bishop of Exeter by John Large		8d
Total	22s	10d

Necessary expenses

Parchment bought for the whole year	7s	6d
Parchment bought for the court of St Michael		4d
One carpenter hired to mend the North Gate at assessment [*ad tax'*]		18d
Spikes bought for the same		12d
Timber and tables bought for the same		4d
One roofer hired with his servants for roofing above the Guildhall for one day's allowance and a half		7d
Wedges and laths bought for the same		2d
Making one shop from new for one butcher together with timber of broom [?brushwood] for covering and carpentry	2s	1d
For the expenses of Mark the clerk riding to the earl to deliver the amercements of Thomas Kyngestone taken by green wax		6d
One horse hired for the same		2d
One seam of firewood bought for burning the false measures		2d

One lock bought for guarding prisoners		3d
One lock bought for the door of the house of Richard Otery to put there a fish table at the time of St Nicholas' fair		3d
To men for binding and carrying the false measures to the Guildhall		4d
Mending the fish tables timber and nails bought for the same		11d
Candles bought		0¾d
Timber bought for trestles to carry the fish tables		2d
Nails bought for mending the aforesaid tables		5d
One carpenter hired for one day and a half to mend the said tables		4½d
One boy hired and sent after Thomas de Kyngestone		1d
Cleaning the Guildhall for Christmas		3d
Straw bought for the same		3½d
200 nails for laths bought for the Guildhall		5d
Two tables, nails, timber and carpentry for mending the fish tables		12d
Expenses of John Lurlegh and John Crittone towards *Colepole* to seize ships		8d
Mending the South Gate timber and spikes bought for the same and carpentry		20d
Sand and nuncheons for the said Gate		5d
Mats bought for the Guildhall		5d
Rushes bought to put in the solar of the Guildhall and in the hall		6d
Cleaning the Guildhall for the feast of St John the Baptist		3d
To the clerk of Exeter Castle for having respite from the amercement of Thomas Kyngestone on the Tuesday next after the feast of the Purification of Blessed Mary	6s	3d
The expenses of John Lurlegh going to Ottery St Mary after Roger Roche		6d
Candles bought for guarding one man in the church of St Petrock at the suit of John Hulle		5d
Total	29s	2¾d

Expenses about the walls of the aforesaid city next to Crikelepytte

Four quarters of lime bought on the Monday next before the feast of St Katherine	4s	
To John Kylmyngtone for the said week following		16d
To Thomas Proute		16d
To John Ballok'		9d
To Edward		6d

To William Rede for Saturday		2d
To Henry Wade for carrying sand for the aforesaid work		4d
Four quarters of lime bought on the following Monday	4s	
To John Kylmyngtone for the said week		20d
To John Mewy		18d
To John Ballok'		11d
To Edward		11d
To Henry Wade for carrying sand for the said week		8d
For nuncheons		3d
In the week next after the feast of St Andrew paid to John Kylmyngtone		22d
To John Mewy		22d
To John Ballok'		14½d
To Edward		14½d
To Henry Wade and his colleague for carrying stones and sand for the aforesaid wall		23d
Beer for the same workers		1d
On the Monday next before the feast of St Thomas for three quarters of lime bought	3s	3d
To John Kylmyngton for the following week	2s	
To John Mewy	2s	
To William Rede		11d
To John Ballok'		15d
To Edward		15d
Nuncheons		5d
To Henry Wade & his colleague with two horses for the whole week	3s	8d
In the week next before Christmas paid to John Kylmyngtone	2s	
To John Mewy	2s	
To William Rede		18d
To John Ballok'		15d
To Edward		15d
Beer for the same		4d
To Benedict Martyn with two horses for five days' allowance		20d
To Walter atte Wode being over the workers		12d
Total	52s	2d

Allowances

Seeks allowance for the amercement of John Swanetone	£8	13s	4d[2]
The amercement of John Molyns		60s[2]	
The amercement of Adam Brasyutere		6s	8d[2]
The amercement of Richard Somaystre			40d[2]

[2] entry crossed through

The amercement of Simon atte Pytte		20d[2]
The amercement of John Beridon		40d[2]
The amercement of Richard Olyver		40d[2]
The amercement of John Somaystre [*seler*]	2s[2]	
The amercement of John Sleghe		40d[2]
The amercement of Nicholas Brittestouwe	40s[2]	
The amercement of John Ayssch		20d[2]
The amercements condoned by the mayor as is shown by the account of John Large	14s	3d[3]
The amercements which are in the fee of St[4] Stephen as is shown by the same account		3d[5]
The amercements of the court of the mayor's tourn and the bakers which cannot be levied as is shown by the account of the aforesaid John	10s	3d[6]
The amercement of Maurice Storde and the amercement of John Brown because they were in the mayor's tourn		3d
The amercements of the underbailiffs		16d
Amercements condoned by the mayor as is shown by the account of Henry Stam		22d
Amercements which cannot be levied as is shown by the account of the aforesaid Henry	11s	2d[7]
Amercements which are in the fee of St Nicholas	2s	8d[8]
The amercements in the fee of St Stephen as is shown by the account of the aforesaid Henry	2s[9]	
Amercements condoned by John Spycere		11d
Condoned by John Swanetone		20d
Amercements condoned by Roger atte Wille as is shown by the account of the aforesaid Henry		4d
Condoned by the seneschals		20d
Amercements condoned by the mayor as is shown by the account of John Lurlegh	9s	7d[10]
Amercements which are in the fee of St Nicholas as is shown [by] the account of the aforesaid John		6d[11]
Condoned by Roger atte Wille		3d
Condoned by John Swanetone		3d
Amercements which cannot be levied as is shown by the account of the aforesaid John Lurlegh		10d[12]
Amercements condoned by the mayor as is shown by the account of John Crittone	3s	2d[13]

[2] entry crossed through
[3] *6d* crossed through
[4] *Nicholas &* crossed through
[5] *3s 7d* crossed through
[6] *11s 5d* crossed through
[7] *13s 2d* crossed through
[8] *2s 8d* crossed through
[9] *3d* crossed through
[10] *8s 2d* crossed through
[11] *2s 4d* crossed through
[12] *6s 4d* crossed through
[13] *8d* crossed through

Amercements condoned by Roger atte Wille		2d
Amercements condoned by John Swanetone		2d
Amercements which are in the fee of St Nicholas		21d[14]
Amercements of Amicia Forlanger in the fee of St Stephen as is shown by the account of the aforesaid John Crittone		3d[15]
Amercements which cannot be levied	6s	1d[16]
Amercement of John Somaystre, dyer, because it is in the mayor's tourn as is shown by the account of the aforesaid John Crittone		3d
Condoned to Adam Kyng' baker by the mayor and community	2s	11d
Pardoned to Richard Olyver by the mayor	2s	
Amercements paid into the pyx as is shown by the account of H. Stam[17]	2s	2d
For having a quittance of the duke of Cornwall from Lostwithiel		6d
Total	79s	3d

[*Dorse*]
Verte in tergo

Sum of all the totals of the discharge of the said
John £67 7s 2½d whence deducted from the sum
of the charge below he owes £32 5s 7d of which
he allows to the same 56s 8d pardoned to John
Molyns for a certain amercement of 60s.[18] Item
allowed to the same £4 13s 4d for his
amercement. And thus he owes £24 15s 7d. And
he has a day to pay the aforesaid cash Monday in
the morrow of St Hilary. And he finds pledges
John Gyst, John Spicer, Richard Oliver, William
Benet, Alexander Oldeston, and John Beridon.
Afterwards allowed to him 5s for Thomas de
Kyyngeston by the mayor and community. And
thus he owes £24 10s 7d.
Afterwards allowed[19] to the same £12 16s 3d paid
to the prior of Holy Trinity London by quittance
for Michaelmas term for the 26th year. And
respited[20] to the same £10 which he says he paid
to the receiver of the lord prince for the farm of
the city aforesaid for the same term by the

[14]*2s 8d* crossed through
[15]*3d* crossed through
[16]*7s 5d* crossed through
[17]line crossed through
[18]*60s* underlined
[19]*paid* crossed through
[20]*allowed* crossed through

quittance which he has not at present. And 2s
paid to the clerk of the said receiver for the
quittance etc. And there are allowed to him 30s
in full payment of 40s which he paid to the earl of
Northampton by order of the mayor. And thus
he owes net except for the £10 respited above
because he did not bring the quittance and 2s for
the clerk's fee for writing the said quittance 2s 4d
which were afterwards placed in the pyx.

1352–3 ACCOUNT OF RICHARD OLYVER OF KINGSTON, SENESCHAL AND RECEIVER OF THE COMMON GOODS OF THE AFORESAID CITY, FROM MICHAELMAS 26 EDWARD III TO THE SAME FEAST 27 [EDWARD III]

Fixed rents

Rents of the aforesaid city and the suburbs of the same city with the rent of *Pratteshide* for the whole year	£7	10d
Rent of the farm of Duryard	£32	
Nothing for the passage because there is no boat		
Total £39		10d

Issues of the city

Custom of fish this year	£8	10s	
Custom of meat this year		30s	
Petty customs		26s	8d
Custom of flour		7s	
Custom of woad		3s	
St Nicholas' fair this year		48s	
Issues of the pyx this year		16s	2½d
Grazing sold at *Crolledych*		5s	
Grazing sold outside the North Gate			20d
Custom of oil		2s	
Custom of wine	£4	12s	4d
Custom of iron and other merchandise as is shown in the court rolls		18s	1d
Custom of bread		3s	
For stalls where the meat was sold		18s	
Bagavel and burgavel		43s	4d
Total £24		4s	3½d

Profits of the courts

Various amercements and fines of the courts as is shown by the court rolls this year	£12	13s	9d[1]
From the mayor's tourn	£4	9s	7d[2]

[1] *5d* crossed through
[2] *11s* crossed through

Amercements of the bakers		21s	6d
Entrants to the freedom this year		60s	
One *panno* waif		20s	
One cup taken from the hands of a thief		10s	
Total	£22	14s	10d
Sum total of the whole charge	£85	19s	11½d

Rent deficits

Tenement of William Harewille within the West Gate	4s	
Vyke tenement in *Maudelynestrete*		20d
The tenement of John Houpere within the North Gate		12d
The tenement of Gilbert Harpour within the North Gate		12d
Three doors called *Hangemannesplace* outside the East Gate		12d
Tenths of the rent of the tenement of *Pratteshude*	2s	2d
The gate of the archdeacon of Cornwall	2s	
The gate formerly of William de Bykelegh now in the hands of the Friars Preachers		6d
Two plots which William de Pontyndone held which lie near to the tenement of the archdeacon of Totnes		16d
The exit at the back part of the tenement of the archdeacon of Totnes	2s	
A certain plot above the North Gate		6d
The tenement formerly of John Rok' in Goldsmith Street	10s	
A plot which William Cogan held between the city walls		1d
A shop which John Screeche holds next to the Guildhall	6s	
A certain plot which John Uphavene held next to the entry of his messuage		1d
A plot of Master Walter Gyffard next to his porch		6d
Tenement of John Dollyng next to the South Gate	3s	
Tenement of Richard Gyffard next to the North Gate	2s	8d
The prior of Plympton for making a certain step in the king's highway next to the Bishop's Gate		4d
A plot which John Dollyng held next to his tenement		12d
A certain beam situate in the king's highway which William Daun held		4d
Rents about the pillory because it is empty	6s	6d[3]
A beam of Richard Colbroukford		4d
A step of Thomas Wyteslegh within the South Gate		8d
Total	48s	8d

[3] 7s crossed through

Rents paid

To the receiver of lord Edward prince of Wales and duke of Cornwall for the rent of the farm of the aforesaid city for Easter and Michaelmas terms as is shown by quittance	£20		
For having a quittance		4s	
To the prior of Holy Trinity London for the farm of the aforesaid city as is shown by quittance	£25	12s	6d
To the parish rectors of the aforesaid city for two terms of the year as of custom		4s	8d
Total	£46		14d

Fees paid

To Robert Brideport mayor of the aforesaid city for his fee for the year	100s	
To the three seneschals for their fees	60s	
To the receiver for the year	40s	
To his clerk	10s	
To Robert atte Weye for his office being recorder and his pension this year	60s	
To Martin the clerk for his fee for the same time	40s	
To the four bailiffs for their fees for a whole year according to the custom of the city	40s	4d
Four robes for the aforesaid bailiffs	48s	
To the four keepers of the gates of the aforesaid city according to the customs of the city	12s	
Bread sent to the mayor, seneschals and other officers *viz* the mayor 14 loaves and the recorder and seneschals to all of them 12 loaves and their clerks five loaves for Christmas according to the custom of the aforesaid city	6s	4d
Wine sent to the same officers *viz* to the mayor[4] four gallons, to recorder and seneschals two gallons, and to the clerk one gallon and not more because the recorder had nothing	10s	
Bread sent to the same officers for Easter	5s	2d
Wine sent to the same for the same feast according to the custom of the aforesaid city	8s	
Four gallons of wine sent at Michaelmas to Robert Brideport mayor in the preceding year and to John Spycer mayor for the year to come	2s	8d
Wine on the mayor's election day four and a half gallons	3s	
Fire on the same day		10d
Total £22	6s	4d

[4]*recorder* crossed through

Foreign payments

To Nicholas Wytyng for his fee this year	20s	
To John Bosoun the community's attorney in the common bench	13s	4d
To Robert Brideport attorney in the lord king's bench for the year	20s	
To William Auncel sheriff of Devon for having respite from £20 which runs upon the community of the aforesaid city	40s	
To the said William in the eve of Easter for goods lately of Robert Hathelsthane by order of the mayor	26s	8d
To the clerk for having quittance		2d
To the said sheriff by the amercement of the bailiffs before William de Schareshull justice of the lord king by order of the mayor	6s	8d
To the rector of the church of St Pancras for a tenth of St Nicholas' fair	2s	
To Richard Forestere bailiff of the lord earl for the third part of the custom of wine belonging to the said earl	30s	9½d
To Robert Brideport mayor for the purchase of one writ to release the city aforesaid from £20 12d	27s	4d
Total £9	6s	11½d

Gifts and presents

Wine sent to William Auncel sheriff of Devon in Lent by order of the mayor on two occasions *viz* one gallon of red wine		18d
Four gallons of wine sent to Richard Borton justice of the lord king in autumn	2s	
Wine sent to the clerk of John de Kendale receiver of the lord prince		12d
To a certain messenger carrying the lord king's writ for parliament for the feast of St Hilary by order of the mayor	2s	
To a certain messenger carrying the lord king's writ of the staple	2s	
To a certain messenger carrying the lord king's writ for parliament for Michaelmas by order of the mayor	2s	
To two other messengers on the same occasion by order of the mayor		6d
Total	11s	

Expenses about the chapel above the East Gate

Ten seams of sand bought		4d
Four quarters of lime bought	3s	
Two hundred wedges bought		3d

Laths bought		5d
250 nails bought for the laths		5d
Three roofers with three servants for one week with nuncheons	7s	5d
300 roofing stones bought		9d
Mending the lock at the chapel aforesaid		1d
Total	12s	8d

Necessary expenses

Parchment bought for the whole year	6s	1d
Buying a lock for the South Gate with one plate of iron bought for the same		4d
Wine given to the taxers of the courts on occasions		10d
Cleaning the Guildhall		1d
Rushes bought for the same for the whole year		4d
To Stephen Crokkernewille for mending the stocks and one key for the Guildhall door		9d
One key bought for the pyx		1d
Ten tables bought for fish tables		15d
Legs [*legges*] for the same		6d
Nails for the same		7½d
To Richard atte Forde for making the stocks for four days' allowance		16d
One other carpenter hired for two days' allowance		8d
Two sawyers hired for one day sawing the stocks		5d
Sand bought for the Guildhall before Christmas		1d
Laths bought		4d
One quarter of lime bought		10d
150 nails bought		3¾d[5]
Wedges bought		2d
350 roofing stones bought for the Guildhall		11½d
Carriage of the said stones towards the Guildhall		1½d
One roofer hired with his servant for one week		20d
Buying one lock for the North Gate		2d
Eight tables bought for the fish stalls		12d
One lock bought for the stocks		3d
To the clerk of Nicholas Pynnok' for carrying a quittance from Cornwall for Michaelmas term of the farm of the aforesaid city	2s	
For tables bought for the shop next to the Guildhall		6d
For nails bought for the same		3d
For a carpenter hired for mending the said shop		3d
One lock bought for the same		4d
Total	22s	6¼d

[5] *4¼d* crossed through

Allowances

Amercements condoned by the mayor and community as is shown by the account of John Large	3s	7d
Amercements in the fee of St Stephen as is shown by the account of the aforesaid John		3d
Amercements which are in the fee of St Nicholas[6]		13d
Condoned by Richard Oliver		12d
Condoned by Thomas Spycere		3d
Condoned by Robert Broun		3d
Amercements which cannot be levied as is shown by the account of the aforesaid John		15d
Amercements condoned by the mayor and community as is shown by the account of John Critton	16s	2d
Amercements in the fee of St Stephen		6d
Amercements which cannot be levied as is shown by the same account	5s	11d
Amercements of John Brounewille because it is in the mayor's tourn		3d
Amercements condoned by the mayor and community as is shown by the account of Randolph Mipeleshale	3s	8d
Amercements because they cannot be levied		12d
Amercement of John Lurleigh		3d
Amercement of Robert Mollond because it is in the mayor's tourn		3d
Amercements condoned by the mayor and community as is shown by the account of Henry Stam	2s	4d
Amercements condoned by John Gyst		13d
Amercements condoned by Richard Olyver		6d
Amercements in the fee of St Stephen		12d
Amercements which are in the fee of St Nicholas		9d
Amercements which cannot be levied as is shown by the account of the aforesaid Henry		20d
Amercement of John Colbrouk condoned by John Spycere mayor		40d
Condoned to the same John by the mayor		5d
Condoned to Richard Horn	2s	10d
From the servant of John Chaundouns		40d
Total	52s	11d
Sum total of all expenses and allowances £85	2s	2¾d

And thus he owes net 17s 8¾d. Afterwards allowed to the same 6d for the amercement of Stephen Bollok condoned by the mayor and community and 2s 2d condoned to Walter Iracle for a certain amercement of 40d

[6]*Stephen* crossed through

condoned by the mayor and community and thus he owes 15s 0¾d and afterwards there are allowed to him 20s for the fine of John Moleys for entry into the freedom pardoned to William de Albe Marlea and thus the total of payments and allowances exceeds the sum of the charge by 5s of which Roger atte Wille receiver following him pays to the same 40d and the same Richard has pardoned 20d.

APPENDIX I: TRANSCRIPT OF THE ACCOUNT FOR 1339–40

Compot' Roberti de Brideport' Spic' Senescalli & Receptor' bonorum
Communium Civitat' Exon' A festo Sancti Michaelis Archangeli Anno
r'r' Edwardi tertii A conquestu Anglie tertiodecimo usque idem festum
Anno revoluto

Onus

Receptio arr'
In primis onerat se de liijs iiijd recept' de arrerag' Compoti Nicholai de
Godiscote Receptor' anni proximi precedent'. Item onerat se de xld
recept' de arr' Johannis de Fenton' de coll' tall' domini reg'.

Summa lvjs viijd

Redd' civitat'
Item onerat se de vj li vjs iiijd recept' de reddit' ass' totius civitat' &
suburb' per idem tempus & de xxv li xijs vjd recept' de firma de Duryerd
de anno & tempore predicti Nicholai & de xxv li xijs vjd recept' de
eadem firma de Duryerd de anno presenti & de xxviijs recept' de Passag'[1]
de Prattyshide & de iiij li recept' de Bagg' & Britth' per idem tempus de
claro.

Summa lxij li xixs iiijd

Exit' civitat' & pastur' vend'
Item onerat se de xj li recept' de cust' Pissium per idem tempus & de xljs
recept' de locatione tabul' cum trestall' & de xlvjs viijd recept' de cust'
carnium per idem tempus & de vjs viij d recept' de cust' pan' & de iijs
recept' de cust' oll' & de xs rec' de cust' Blad' & farine & de ijs rec' de
cust' Ways' abduct' de civitate & de liiijs iiijd recept' de minut' cust' &
de vjd rec' de pastur' vend' infra portam borialem & Wyndesore & de ijs
rec' pro pastur' inter portam borial' & portam oriental' ex parte
exteriori[2] & xxixs rec' de cust' vinorum applic' apud Toppisham per idem
tempus & de xixs[3] rec' de cust' Wayd' sepium & all' ac al'
mercimoniorum applic' ibidem per idem tempus & de ijs vjd rec' de
cust' furrur'.[4]

Summa xxj li xvijs vjd ob'

Extractus & perquis' cur'
Item onerat se de xiij li xiiijs[5] recept' de extract' Turnorum maior' ut pat'

[1] *& domo* above line
[2] entry underlined
[3] *ixd ob'* above line
[4] *de civitat' abductarum* in different ink
[5] *xjd* above line

per compot' seriantorum & de x li xxijd recept' de extract' cur' idem
tempus ut pat' per comp' dictorum seriantorum & de ixs xd recept' de
amerciament' pistorum & de xj li viijs[6] rec' de finibus factis per idem
tempus & de x li xijs viijd rec' ingredient' lib' per idem tempus & de xxijs
iijd ob' rec' de exit' Pixid' per idem tempus & de xvjs vjd rec' de catall'
felonum per idem tempus & de xld rec' pro uno equo invento Woyf'.

Summa xlviij li ixs xjd ob'

Rec' for'
Item onerat se de xviijs rec' pro loc' habendis in Gyald' tempore Numnd'
(?) in festo sancti Nicholai hoc anno. Item onerat se de x li rec' de ingress'
pro vendic' porte Austral'[7] & iiij li xs rec' de Willelmo de Kydelond' pro
firma molend' de Crykelepitt'. Item onerat se de vjd pro cineribus
plumb' vend'.[8]

Summa cviijs vjd
Summa summarum totius oneris cxlj li xjs

Exonus

Resolut' redd'
Inprimis idem comput' solut' Priori & conventui sancte Trinitat' Lond'
ut pat' per acquietanc' xxv li xijs vjd de Tempore Nicholai de Godiscote
Receptor' anni proximi precendent'. Item comput' solut' eisdem Priori &
conventui ut pat' in eadem acquiet' x li de arr' dicti redd' sibi aretro
existent' de eodem anno. Item comput' solut' eisdem Priori & conventui
xij li xvjs iijd de Termino Pasch' anni present' vid' anno xiiij[mo] ut pat' per
acquietanc'. Item comput' solut' eisdem Priori & conventui xij li xvjs iijd
de Termino sancti Michaelis eiusdem anni ut pat' per acquiet'. Item
comp' solut' eisdem Priori & conventui x li de arr' dicti redd' dicti anni
presentis in plenar' solutionem omnium arr' de dicto redd' annual' sibi
tunc debit' ut pat' per eorum acquiet'. Item comput' solut' Receptori
domini ducis Cornub' pro feod' firma civitat' vid' de termino Pasch' anni
present' ut pat' per acquiet' x li & de termino sancti Michaelis eiusdem
anni ut pat' per aliam acquiet' x li. Item comp' solut' domino com'
Devon' de tertia parte vinorum applic' apud Toppisham per idem
tempus ixs viijd. Item comp' solut' rector' civitat' pro reddit' Gyald' iiijs
viijd.

xx
Summa iiij xj xixs iiijd

Defect' redd'
Item comput' in defect' redd' civitat' v' De Ten' Willelmi de Doune[9] quia
non potest dist'. De domo Willelmi Peverel quod Willelmus Vyke aliqu'
tenuit in maudelynestret' quia prostr' xxd.[10] De uno hostio extra port'
orient' quod Robertus de Wotton' ten' pro eodem iiijd.[11] De quadam
placea domini Johannis Eysi exopposito venell' omnium sanctorum in

[6]*vijd* above line
[7]entry crossed through
[8]entry in different ink
[9]*vijs* crossed through; *vjd* above line
[10]entry crossed through
[11]entry crossed through

Aurifabria pro eodem vj d. De quadam venell' ibid' abstructa quam
idem dominus Johannes occupat pro eodem ijs. De quadam porta
Willelmi de Bykeleygh' nunc fratrum predicatorum vjd pro eodem. De
port' quam Henr' Bollek' quondam Archidiaconus Cornub' tenuit pro
eodem ijs. De duabus placeis terr' iacentibus iuxta ten' Archidiaconi
Totton' quas Willelmus de Puntyngdon' quondam tenuit pro eodem xvjd.
De quodam exit' in posteriori parte ten' eiusdem archidiaconi Totton'
pro eodem ijs. De quadam placea supra portam Borialem quam Rector
ecclesie sancti Pauli ten' pro eodem vjd. De Priore de Plympton' pro
quodam gradu figend' in regia strat' quia removeatur iiijd.[12] De clausu
Johannis de Chuddeleygh' iuxta port' Episcopi quia non potest distr' vjd.
De scopa iuxta Gyald' quam Nicholaus Coppe tenuit xs. De scop' in
Pillor' quia non occ' ijs. Item pet' alloc' de xs condonat' firmar' custum'
pisc' per maior' & communitatem hoc anno.[13]

    Summa xxxjs iiijd

Alloc' seriant'
Item comput' de divers' alloc' seriantorum ut pat' in comp' eorum tam
de Turnis maioris quam de extract' cur' vid' de amerciam' cond' ut pat'
in quatuor comp' suis de Turnis predictis vij li xvijs. Item de amerc' q'
levari non possunt ut pat' in eisdem comp' de dictis turnis xxvjs ijd. Item
de amerc' levand' de divers' feod' ut pat' in dictis comp' suis xxijs xd.
Item de amerc' errat'[14] & al' minut' alloc' ut p' in eisdem comp' suis de
predictis Turnis xxxvijs jd. Item comp' de amerc' cond' ut pat' in
quatuor comp' dictorum seriantorum de extract' omnium cur' vj li xiijd.
Item comp' de amerc' q' levari non possunt ut pat' in eisdem comp' suis
de dictis extract' cur' xvs vd. Item comp' de amerc' Levand' de divers'
Feod' ut pat' in dictis comp' suis de eisdem extract' cur'.[15] Item comp' de
amerc' errat' &[16] & al' minut' alloc' ut pat' per eosdem comp' xiiijs xjd
ob'.

Item petit alloc' de Cs un' receptor oneratur in extractis Johannis de
Conyngtr' de amerc' cur' quos Thomas de Lytchyffeld tunc maior civitat'
ex consensu & ad rogat' Hamonis de Dyrworth & al' proborum totaliter
condonavit Edwardo atte Stone.[17]

    Summa xix li xiiijs vjd ob'

Expens' necessar'
Item comp' solut' pro viij Duoden' Bord' de Popl' pro tabul' faciend' ad
pistar' prec' duod' xijd quod extendit ad viijs. Item in ij duod' huiusmodi
bord' empt' pro eodem prec' duod' xvjd[18] quod extendit ijs viijd. Item
solut' ad portand' omnes eosdem Bord' ad Gyald' ijd. Item in ij dol' &
di' vacuis empt' pro legg' ad easdem tabul' faciend' xvd. Item in x^c clav'

---

[12]entry crossed through
[13]entry in different ink
[14]*et sub ped' comp' cond'* above line
[15]entry crossed through
[16]*sub ped' comp' cond'* above line; *al'* crossed through
[17]entry crossed through
[18]*xvjd* underlined

ad eadem Legg' firmand ad tabul' & pro tabul' prec' C iijd[19] ijs vjd. In ijᶜ clav' ad idem prec'[20] prec' C iiijd[21] viijd. Item in vij parvis Lignis de querco empt' de Johanne Somayst' pro trestall' inde faciend' prec' ligni jd ob'[22] xd ob'. Item in portacionem eorundem ad Gyald' jd. Item in uno ligno de suo proprio de querco iiijd. Item in locationem ij carpont' die sabbati prox' ante cynerum mercur' pro tabul' & trestall' faciend' sumens uterque per eandem diem cum pot' eorum ijd ob' qua'[23] vd ob'. In locac' j carpont' per eandem diem pro eodem cum pot' suo iiijd qua'. In ij sarrat' eodem die cum pot' eorum vd ob'. In locat' iij carpont' pro eodem die Lune sequent' sumens quilibet per diem illum cum pot' eorum iijd qua'[24] ixd ob' qua'. In loc' iij carpont' pro eodem die quibus per diem cum pot' ijd ob' qua'[25] viijd qua'. In ij sarrat' eodem die cum pot' eorum vd ob'. Item die mart' prox' sequent' in Loc' omnium & singul' eorundem operar' eodem modo ut pat' particulariter in eodem die lune quod extend' ad xxiijd ob'. Item in loc' iij carpont' die mercur' prox' sequent' pro eodem quibus cum pot' eodem die iijd qua'[26] ixd ob' & qua'. In j carpont' eodem die pro eodem cum pot' suo ijd ob' qua'. In ij sarrator' eodem die cum potu eorum vd ob'. In j carpont' die iov' prox' sequent' cum pot' suo iijd qua'. In ij sarrator' eodem die cum pot' vd ob'. In j carpont' die veneris sequent' cum pot' iijd qua'. In j carpont' die sabbati prox sequent' ijd. In vj votmell' vij li plumbi empt' pro penticio Gyald' cooperiᵈ' prec' votmel' ijs jd[27] quod extendit ad xijs viijd. In iiijᵒʳ summis bosci ad idem vijd ob'. In loc' plumbatoris pro dicto plumbo & vij votmell' de veteri plumbo de dicto penticio faciend' & componend' vid' pro factur' cuiusl' votmel' iiijd[28] quod extendit ad iijs iijd. Item pro pot' suo per idem tempus operis iiijd. Item in una C clav' & di' ad idem iiijd. In portacionem dictorum vj votmel' de domo Reg' Wython' usque ad Gyald' jd. Item in una serrura pro host' communis ciste empt' cum j clav' & clavibus ad idem xd. In emend' unius serur' ad port' Australem ijd. In emend' unius parietis supra ponde' dicte porte ijd. In j serur' empt' pro host' celar Gyald' jd. In emend' unius serur' pro exteriori host' eiusdem celar' jd. In ij bord' empt' & in emend' unius schop' in pill' viijd. In emend' communis pixid' jd. In stramine ad Gyald' per vices iiijd. In una serur' empt' pro communi fonte civitat' jd. Item comp' pro j clave empt' pro port' occid' ijd.

Summa xliiijs iijd qua'

Expn' & solut' forins'
Item comp' solut' Roberto de Bridep' attornato communitatis in banco pro interesse suo pro civitate in parliam' tent' apud Westm' in xvᵃ sancti

---

[19] *iijd* underlined
[20] *prec'* crossed through
[21] *iiijd* underlined
[22] *jd ob* underlined
[23] *ijd ob' qua'* underlined
[24] *iijd qua'* underlined
[25] *ijd ob' qua'* underlined
[26] *iijd qua'* underlined
[27] *ijs jd* underlined
[28] *iiijd* underlined

Hillar' di' marc'. Item comp' solut' eidem Roberto pro interesse ibid' in parliam' tent' in medio quadrag' di' marc'. Item Thome de Crauthorne pro eodem tunc temporis xjs vjd. Item comp' solut' iiij^{or} hominibus pro eorum interesse ibid' in quodam communi consilio circa festum assumptionis beate Mar' xxxvjs. Item compt' solut' dicto Roberto pro eodem ibid' in parliam' tento ante festum sancti Michaelis j marc'. Item Radulpho Speek' pro eodem tunc temporis di' marc'. Item solut' Johanni de Bruton ad recordand' unum attornat' pro civitate in banco di' marc'. Item comp' solut' domino Johanni de Raleygh' de Beaud' tunc vic' Devon' de reman' fin' pro confirmatione carte libertat' civitat' habend' sicut idem vic' habuit in precept' per breve domini reg' cxs ut pat' per acquietanc'. Item solut' pro un' littera deferend' attornat' communitatis in scaccario domini r' iijd. Item solut' pro inspectione carte libertat' civitat' apud Lond' vjd. Item solut' uno garcioni deferent' litteras apud Wyncestr' Salm' & alibi ad inspicien' quid ibi factum fuerat de tall' domini reg' v' de ix^a parte &c' viijd. Item solut' Willelmo de Milton pro divers' brevibus perpetrand' versus dominum Willelmum Cheyny pro exonerari de quodam antiquo debito vjs vjd. In j equo Loc' pro Alexandro Oldeston' equitant' versus Cherd ad just' ibid' ass' pro litteris eis deferend' pro communibus negoc' & in expenc' suis xvjd. Item in j equo loc' pro Simone le Taverner equitand' versus Toppisham pro un' nav' de Yernemouth arrestand' & in expens' suis ibid' iijd. Item comp' solut' uno homini ad portant' apud Lond' xxv li xijs vjd de redd' Trinitat' Lond' de tempore Nicholai de Godyscote rec' anni prox' precedent' xld. Item solut' uno homini ad portand' ibid' postmod' x li de arrerag' tunc de eodem anno solvend' xld. Item comp' solut' uno homini ad portand' ibid' xxv li xijs vjd de redd' predicto pro toto anno presenti vid' per duas vices portant' di' marc'.

Summa xj li iiijd

Dona & exhennia
Item comp' in don' & exhenniis per precept' maioris vid'
In primis in[29]

Item miss' domino expiscopo Exon' apud Clyst' in adventu suo ibid' de parliament' tento ultimo die Octobr' apud Lond'. In uno carcos' bov' iijs. In vj carcos' ov' iij s. In vj pertic' xjd. In vj gall' bosci iiijd. In iij lag' musc' & j quart' xviijd. In j equo loc' pro dicto exhenn' portand' jd ob'. In pan' & vino miss' domino Johanni de Ralegh' de Charles vic' Devon' de novo constitut' xixd. In vino miss' Hamoni de Dyrworth' in recessu suo de Exon' versus cur' pro serianto ordinar' vjd. In pan' & vino miss' eidem in primo adventu suo Exon' postmod' ijs iiijd. In pan' & vino miss' domino Jacobo de Cokygnton' un' coll' x^e domino r' concess' pro respectu inde habend' xiiijd. In pan' & vino miss' Math'o de Crauthorne altero coll' eiusdem x^e pro eodem viijd. Verte in dorso de eodem panell' In pan' & vino misso vic' Devon' pro respect' habendo de quodam brevi ad distr' communitat' pro arr' redd' Trinitat' Lond' xvd. In pan' & vino miss' domino Willelmo de Scharishill' just' domini reg' in cessione ass' in quadrag' xxijd. In pan' & vino miss' domino Johanni Inge tunc temporis

[29]Gap in account

xxijd. In pan' & vino miss' domino Jacobo de Wodestok' tunc temporis
xxijd. In pan' & vino miss' Hamoni de Dyrworth' in eadem cessione xijd.
In vino miss' dicto domino Jacobo de Wodestok in advent' suo Exon' de
Cornub' postmod' xijd. In vino miss' domini vic' pro auxilio prestand' in
prima cessione just' de Treyllebast' xijd. In vino miss' Johanni de
Stouford' un' just' de Treylleb' vj d. Item solut' clerico dictorum just' de
Treyll' pro carta libertat' civitat' allocand' ijs. In xij pertic' & in vino
miss' domino episcopo Exon' pro colloquio & consil' suo habendo de tall'
& aliis negoc' communibus iijs vijd. In vino miss' Hamoni de Dyrworth'
in recessu suo de Exon' versus cur' post pasch' vjd. In pan' & vino miss'
capital' collector' tall' domini reg' de ixª sibi concess' iijs ixd. In vino
miss' vic' Devon' venient' Exon' de cur' ixd. In vino miss' Hamoni de
Dyrworth' in recessu suo versus cur' ad terminum Trinitat' ixd. In vino
miss' Jacobo de Cokyngton' & Math'o de Crauthorne capital' collector'
xᵉ domino regi concess' quando receperunt compot' de quarterio Austral'
Civitat' xd. In pan' & vino miss' domino Thome Crosse ven' Exon' xixd.
In vino miss' domino Jacobo de Wodestok' just' domini reg' in cessione
just' ass' in autumpno apud Exon' xd. In pan' & vino miss' eidem adhuc
in eadem cessione xvjd. In pan' & vino miss' domino Johanni Inge just'
soc' suo xvjd. In vino miss' eidem similiter in eadem cessione xijd. Item in
vino misso Hamoni de Dyrworth' tunc temporis xijd. In vino miss' dicto
domino Jacobo de Wodestok' in advent' suo de Cornub' Exon' xd. In
vino miss' Hamoni de Dyrworth' in eodem advent' suo de Cornub' xd. In
vino miss' cuidam Rogero Norman ven' Exon' cum commissione reg' pro
nav' perpetrand' ad flotam domini r' xd. Item dat' clerico suo secundum
ordinacionem maior' & probiorum civitat' xld. In pan' & vino miss'
domino Exon' Episcopo die quo probi civitat' fuerant secum ad commest'
Exon' secundum eandem ordinacionem iijs. In vino miss' Johanni de
Stouford in advent' suo Exon' parum ante festum sancti Michaelis xd.
Item comp' solut' pluribus divers' nunciis ven' Exon' de divers' placeis
domini reg' per divers' vic' hoc anno iiijs. Item dat' operar' domini
comit' Devon' apud Exem'r per precept' maior' ad pot' iiijd. In vino
miss' adhuc Hamoni de Dyrworth' in advent' suo Exon' circiter festum
sancti Michaelis vjd.

Summa lviijs ob'

Feodi solut' & pensiones
Item comp' solut' maiori hoc anno pro feod' suo cs. Item comp' solut'
tribus sen' pro feod' suis hoc anno lxs. Item recept' civitat' pro eodem xls.
Item Roberto de Lucy capitali ballivo pro eodem lxs. Item subclerico pro
eodem xxs. Item iiijᵒʳ seriantibus pro eodem xls iiijd. Item quatuor
janitor' portarum pro eodem xijs. Item comp' solut' in exhenn' miss'
maior' & senescall' & aliis probis vill' ad festum natal' domini secundum
consuetudinem civitat' xs ijd. Item in exhenn' miss' eidem ad festum
pasch' vijs. Item in exhenn' miss' tam novis offic' quam antiquis die
electionis nove maioris & sen' vs iiijd. Item comp' solut' Bartholomaeo
atte Mede communi attornato in communi banco domini r' pro pensione
sua hoc anno xxs. Item comp' solut' Roberto de Brideport' attornat'
communitat' in banc' domini r' pro eodem xxs. Item comp solut' clerico
suo pro omnibus rebus officium suum tangent' per tot' annum scribend'

& pro compot' suo componend' xs. Item comp' in pargamen' empto per
totum annum vs & pro caust' viijd.

   Summa xx li xs vjd
       Summa Summ' omnium expens' & solut'
       Cxlix li xviijs iiijd qua'
Et sic excedit summa expens' summam totius r'
in viij li vjs iiijd qua'

APPENDIX II:
RELATED DOCUMENTS

I

1302–1303 RENTAL OF THE CITY OF EXETER MADE AT THE TERM OF ST MICHAEL IN THE 31ST YEAR OF KING EDWARD (ECA, Miscellaneous Roll 2, No. 28)

Henry de Esse for the farm of Duryard for the year	£25	12s	6d[1]
Henry de Triccote and John le Perour for the tenements which they hold at the West Gate within the walls		7s	6d
Tenements *viz* two shops [*seldis*] which the rector of Holy Trinity holds at the South Gate		8s	
One shop which William Home holds there			
One shop which was Robert Blaunchecote's at the Broadgate [*Brodeyete*]			6d
Hemelin le Gaunter for one tenement within the West Gate		4s	
The tenement which John de la Heye holds there		4s	
The house of the abbot of Tavistock which Robert de Nymeton holds in South Street			4d[2]
Walter le Carpunter for a certain plot at Bishop's Gate			4d[3]
William Peverel's house outside the South Gate in *Maudeleynestret* which Vyk now holds			20d
The house of John le Hopere within the North Gate next to the wall			12d
The house which Gilbert le Harpeur now holds there			12d
The house of Richard Smith [*Fabri*] outside the North Gate			12d
The tenement which Roger Garlaund holds outside the North Gate		3s	
The tenement which Richard Vykeri holds outside the North Gate near to the wall with a certain plot adjoining		6s[4]	
Three doors outside the East Gate opposite *la Crosse*			12d

[1] *Empty because it belongs to the City of London* in margin
[2] line crossed through
[3] line crossed through; *empty because elsewhere* in margin
[4] *J. Soumayst' holds it and the charge is elsewhere* in margin

A certain acre of land which Walter de Langedene
now holds outside the East Gate which formerly
was I. de Exton's   12d

A gate which was formerly William de Bykelegh's
which is now in the hands of the Friars Preachers   6d[5]

The house of Thomas de Chaggeford and Joan his
wife in the High Street of the city   6d

A certain lane next to the house of the same
Thomas there   2s

A gate which Henry de Bollek' formerly archdeacon
of Cornwall held   2s

Two plots which William de Puntyngton held
which adjoin near to the site now of Thomas de
Churleton archdeacon of Wells   16d

The exit in the back part of the tenement of the
archdeacon of Totnes   2s

A certain plot above the North Gate which Thomas
le Spicer holds   6d

The tenement which was Ralph le Slegh's which
William the said archdeacon now holds in
Goldsmith Street   10s

A certain new tenement which John Incheheye has
now built at the West Gate near the church of All
Hallows   4s[6]

The passage of *Pratteside*[7]   30s[8]

The tenement which William Gegyn formerly held
between his tenement and the city wall   1d

The tenement of William de Gatepath next to the
Guildhall for siting a certain wall of a garden   1d

A tenement which John Gerveis occupied outside
the East Gate near the way of the said gate newly
constructed   3s

A certain area outside the East Gate near the
tenement of William Wodekempe now built
which Stephen son of Richard le Peleter and
Robert his brother now hold   6d[9]

The rent of assize of those coming from the pillory
at the four terms of the year   13s

One[10] shop next to the *pretorium* of the Guildhall on
the west side   20s[11]

A certain area which Walter son of Henry[12] Le
Carpenter holds next to the bishop of Exeter's gate   12d[13]

[5]Cross in left hand margin and *Not charged in the first year* in the right hand margin relates to
this and the next five entries, which are bracketed.

[6]Entry underlined and *Supra* written in left hand margin

[7]*From the house nothing 5th year* in right hand margin

[8]*40s* crossed through

[9]*Not charged the first year* in margin

[10]*Two* crossed out

[11]*24s* crossed out

[12]*Walter* crossed out

[13]*Increase from the 8th year* in margin

A certain shop which John le Roper holds in an
unused [*otioso*] area next to the sergemarket
[*sargeriam*]   4s[14]

A certain shop which Henry le Cotiller holds next
to the same on the east side   18d

A certain shop which John le Cotiller holds there
nearer on the east side   18d

A certain shop which Pagan le Bruwere holds there   12d

A certain shop which Ralph le Neldere holds there
on the corner   12d

A certain shop which John Oure holds there on the
other side in the entrance to *fishfoldesyete* on the
corner   4s[15]

A certain shop which Henry le Gaunter held there   8s[16]

A certain shop which Walter de Merton holds near
there   12d

A certain shop which Michael le Cotiller holds near
the shop of Thomas de Codelep   2s

A certain plot which Master John de Uphavene
holds next to the entrance to his messuage   1d

A certain palace [*palacia*] of Master Walter Giffard[17]   6d[18]

John Dollyng next to the South Gate   3s

William le Vychelere of Okehampton for a certain
plot next to the North Gate next to the tenement
which was Gilbert le Harpour's   2s   8d

The farm of the[19] rent of Duryard   £25   12s   6d

A certain tenement which William le Marchal holds
outside the South Gate next to the tenement of
John Dollying   4s[20]

The Prior of Plympton for having an easement in
the king's highway at the said prior's tenement
next to the Bishop's Gate for making a certain
step in the said highway   4d[21]

William le Marchal for a certain plot on the west
side of his shop outside the South Gate   12d

John Dollyng for a certain plot outside the same
gate behind his tenement towards the common
walls   12d[22]

Roger Douste for a tenement granted to him by
charter of the mayor and community at *Pratteside*   8s[23]

---

[14]*because John died William . . . took the same at Michaelmas in the 17th year* written above
[15]*12d* crossed through
[16]*2s before the 7th year and thus quit of 6s* in margin
[17]*This rent was lacking £7 6s 11d* in margin
[18]*1d* crossed through
[19]*whole* crossed through; entry in right hand margin
[20]*As appears by indenture from the increase at the feast of St Michael* in margin
[21]*for the year at the feast of St Michael* in margin
[22]*as appears by indenture* written above the line
[23]*Increase in rent* in margin

John le Somayster *deghe* for a certain plot granted to
the same by the mayor and community which
Roger Beyvyn once held[24]   40d

The same John for a certain plot outside the
aforesaid gate opposite the aforesaid plot towards
the west   40d

A plot of John de Chuddelegh   12d

II

1341–1342 ACCOUNT OF ROBERT LE TAVERNER RECEIVER
OF THE MURAGE GRANTED TO THE CITIZENS OF
THE CITY OF EXETER FROM THE MONDAY AFTER
THE FEAST OF SS SIMON AND JUDE THE
APOSTLES 15 EDWARD III [29 OCTOBER 1341] TO
THE . . . DAY AFTER THE FEAST OF . . . THEN NEXT
FOLLOWING (ECA, Miscellaneous Roll 6)

Charge

For his arrears of his last account for the previous
year for this murage, as is shown at the foot of the
same account   £6   5s   1d

Murage of wine landed at Topsham for the same
time, as is shown in the city customs rolls   36s

Murage of woad, fish, and all other merchandise
landed there for the same time, as is shown in the
same rolls   £4   4s   9d

                                    Total with arrears   £12   5s   10d

Henry Guel and Richard le Hoper skinner
collectors of the murage both of the East Gate
and of the South Gate for 37 weeks, as is shown
by two tallies made between them, at 4s per week   £7   8s

Stephen atte Wode collector of the murage of the
West Gate for 38 weeks at 4s per week, as is
shown by one tally made between them   £7   12s

Gilbert de Dureyerd collector of the murage of the
North Gate, as is shown by his account returned
to the mayor and bailiff   44s   10d

Sale of stones at the common quarry for the whole
of the aforesaid time   41s   10d

Which various men have given in the silver in aid of
the road at Bolehill   6s   10d

                                             Total   £19   13s   6d

Total of the whole charge   £31   19s   4d

---

[24]*outside the North Gate* crossed through

Discharge

Purchase of the commission of the present murage	16s	
Total	16s	

Various expenses about the upkeep of the city walls and also about the quarry and conduit and about repair of the city roads and other necessary works by order of the mayor, as is shown particularly below, *viz*

Next week after the feast of St Martin [10 November], which was the first week of expenditure of the second commission

50 [seams of] sand		15d
three masons to whom 14d for the week, working next to the church of All Hallows on the Walls	3s	6d
one mason for the week		12d
one servant of theirs for the week		8d
transport of water and stone		3d
two men with two horses for 3½ days, each 3d a day		21d
four men at the quarry to whom 8d for the week	2s	8d
their drink by order of the mayor		3d
one barrow (*Berewe*) bought		1d
Total	11s	5d

Week then next following

1½ quarters of sand bought, price 7½d a quarter		11¾d
three masons for the week to whom 14d	3s	6d
one mason for the week		12d
one servant of theirs for the week		8d
transport of water and stone		5d
one man with one horse for 1 day		3d
four men at the quarry to whom 8d for the week	2s	8d
their drink		3d
Total	9s	8¾d

Week then next following in which was the feast of St Andrew [30 November]

1½ quarters of sand, price 7½d a quarter		11¾d
3½ quarters of lime, price 4d a quarter		14d
three masons for the week to whom 14d	3s	6d
one mason for the week		12d

one servant of theirs for the week	8d
transport of water and stone	2d
one man with one horse carrying stone etc. for 2 days, 3d a day	6d
three men at the quarry to whom 7d for the week	21d
their drink	3d

Total	9s	5¾d

Week following in which was the feast of St
Nicholas [6 December]

three masons for the week to whom 12d	3s	
their servant for the week		8d
transport of water and stone		1½d
one man with one horse carrying stone etc. for 1½ days, 3d a day		5d
two men at the quarry for the week, each 7d		14d
their drink		2d

Total	5s	6½d

Week then next following, next to *Wyndesor*

four masons to whom 12d for the week	4s	
their servant for the week		8d
one man with one horse carrying stone for 3 days, 3d a day		9d
transport of water and stone		2d
two men at the quarry, each 8d for the week		16d
their drink		2d

Total	7s	1d

Week next following, *viz* the next whole week before
Christmas, in which was the feast of St Thomas
the Apostle [21 December]

four masons hired to mend a defect in the wall at piece-work	2s	
their servant for the week		7d
one man with one horse for 1½ days, 3d a day		5d
transport of water and stone		2d
two men at the quarry, each 7d for the week		14d
their drink		2d
mending the road at *Bolehill* by order of the mayor		2½d
mending one *bitell*,[1] *viz* iron and working		8½d
making one pick-axe (*picos*) from new, iron and working		8d
one barrow bought		1d

[1] probably a 'beetle' (ramming tool)

timber bought from R. Trobrigge for the conduit etc. with the carpenter's wages		2s	6d
firewood bought	½d		
beef tallow (*sep' bov'*)	12d		
pitch (*pyth'*) and rope	1½d		
solder for mending the said conduit	7d } total	2s	4½d
the plumber's wages for 4 days, 3½d day with his drink	14d		
his servant's wages for the same time	4d		
	Total	11s	0½d

Next week after the feast of St Gregory the Pope in the 16th year [12 March 1342]

hire of six men at the quarry for the week to whom 9d		4s	6d
hire of two women transporting stone and earth for the week, each 6d			12d
their drink for the same			3d
	Total	10s	4d

Week then next following

hire of six men at the quarry working at piece-work for 4 days		3s	6d
hire of two men in the same place in the same way for the same time			10d
their drink			3d
	Total	4s	7d

Next whole working week after Easter

46 quarters of lime bought for stock, price 3½d a quarter with carriage		13s	5d
hire of three masons to deliver stone at the quarry for the week to whom 17d		4s	3d
hire of one mason in the same way in the same place for the week			16d
hire of six men at the quarry digging stones for the week to whom 9d		4s	6d
hire of one man in the same way in the same place for the week			7d
their drink			3d
	Total	24s	4d

Week then next following

hire of two masons working in the same way still at the quarry for the week, each 12d		2s	10d
hire of two masons working in the same way in the same place for 1 day, each 3d a day			6d
their drink for the week by order of the mayor			5d

hire of six men digging at the quarry for the week to whom 9d	4s	6d
hire of one man in the same place digging for the week		7d
their drink		3d
hire of one man with one horse carrying stone at the wall for 5 days, 3¼d a day		16¼d
withies (*vigul'*) bought for mending the barrows		1d
Total	10s	6¼d

Week then next following in which was the feast of
St Mark the Evangelist [25 April]

hire of two masons working at the quarry as above for the week, each 17d	2s	10d
hire of two masons working at the wall[2] for the week, each 16d	2s	8d
their servant for the week		9d
their drink by order of the mayor		4d
hire of five men digging at the quarry for the week to whom 9d	3s	9d
hire of one man digging in the same place for the week		7d
their drink		3d
1 fotmel of lead bought for mending the East Gate	2s	
solder for the same — 10d } *Total*		13d
beef tallow, firewood, moss — 3d } *Total* (*mus'*), and nails		
wages of the plumber and his servant for maintenance of the said Gate with lead at piece-work		15d
Total	15s	6d

Week next following in which were the feasts of SS
Simon and Jude [*recte* Philip and James] and the
Invention of the Holy Cross [3 May]

100 seams of sand bought for stock	2s	6d
hire of three masons working next to *Wyndesor* to whom 14½d for the week because of the said feasts	3s	7½d
hire of two masons working in the same place for the week for that purpose, each 13½d	2s	3d
their drink for that purpose		3d
their servant for that week		7½d
hire of four men digging at the quarry for that week to whom 7½d	2s	6d
hire of one man in the same place for the week		6d

²*in the same place* crossed through

their drink	3d
hire of one man with one horse carrying stone	
at at the wall for 3½ days, 3½d a day	12¼d
transport of water at the wall for making	
mortar there	1d

Total	13s	7¼d

Week next following in which were the feasts of St
John before the Latin Gate [6 May] and the
Ascension [9 May]

as many masons and other workmen and the same prices as the week next preceding, which comes to		11s	1¼d
two barrows bought	2d		
one iron wedge newly made	4½d } total		9½d
mending tools	3d		

Total	11s	10¾d

Week then next following

100 seams of sand	2s	6d
hire of three masons still working at the wall in		
the north quarter for the week to whom 17d	3s	9d
hire of two masons in the same place, each 16d		
for the week	2s	8d
their servant for the week		9d
their drink also by order of the mayor		5d
hire of four men digging at the quarry for the		
week to whom 9d	3s	
hire of one man in the same place for the week		7d
their drink		3d
hire of one man with one horse carrying stone		
at the wall for 5 days, 3½d a day		19¾d

Total	15s	6¾d

Week then next following in which was the feast of
Pentecost [19 May][3]

hire of four masons for 2½ days to whom 3d a		
day	2s	8d
their servant for the same time		4½d
their drink		2d
hire of four men at the quarry for 2½ days,		
1½d a day		18d
hire of one man in the same place for the same		
time		4d
their drink		2d

Total	5s	2½d

[3] *Corporis & sang' Xpi* crossed through

Week then next following in which was the feast of
Corpus Christi [30 May]

hire of three masons still in the north quarter at the wall for the week to whom 17d	4s	3d
hire of two masons for the week, each 16d	2s	8d
their servant for the week		9d
their drink		5d
hire of four men at the quarry to whom for the week 9d	3s	
hire of one man in the same place for the week		7d
their drink		3d
hire of one man with one horse for 4½ days, 3d a day		15¾d
mending various tools		2½d
one rope bought for drawing water at the quarry		1½d
Total	13s	6¾d

Next whole week before the feast of St Barnabas [11
June]

two masons still in the north quarter, each 17d for the week	2s	10d
one mason for the week		16d
one mason for 3 days, 3d a day		9d
one servant for the week		9d
transport of water and stone for the week		4½d
their drink by order of the mayor		5d
six men at the quarry to whom 9d for the week	4s	6d
one man in the same place for the week		7d
their drink		3d
Total	11s	9½d

Week following in which was the feast of St
Barnabas

150 seams of sand, price	3s	9d
two masons, each 17d for the week	2s	10d
one mason for the week		16d
their servant for the week		9d
their drink		5d
six men at the quarry to whom 9d for the week	4s	6d
one man in the same place for the week		7d
their drink		3d
one sieve bought		1d
one large rope bought		5d
Total	14s	11d

Next week before the feast of the Nativity of St John
  [24 June]

50 [seams of] sand		15d
three masons to whom 17d for the week	4s	3d
one mason for the week		16d
their servant for the week		9d
their drink		5d
transport of water and stone		3½d
hire of one man with one horse carrying stone etc. for 5½ days, 3½d a day		18¾d
six workmen at the quarry to whom 9d for the week	4s	6d
one workman in the same place for the week		7d
their drink		4d
Total	15s	3¼d

Week next following in which were the feasts of the
  Nativity of St John and SS Peter and Paul the
  Apostles [29 June]

b—four masons for that week to whom 14½d	4s	10d
d—their drink		4d
c—their servant		7½d
a—50 [seams of] sand		15d
transport of water		1½d
six men at the quarry for that week to whom 7½d	3s	9d
one man in the same place for the week		7d
one man in the same place for 3½ days at piece-work		5d
their drink		3d
Total	12s	2d

Next whole week after the Nativity of St John

34 quarters of lime bought for stock, price 4d a quarter with carriage	11s	4d
100 seams of sand	2s	6d
three masons for the week to whom 17d	4s	3d
one mason for the week		16d
their servant for the week		9d
their drink		5d
transport of water and stone		4d
hire of six men at the quarry to whom 9d for the week	4s	6d
hire of one man in the same place for the week		7d
their drink because they were more		4d
Total	26s	5d

Week next following in which was the feast of the
  Translation of St Thomas the Martyr [3 July]

100 [seams of] sand	2s	6d
two masons for the week, each 17d	2s	10d
one mason for the week		16d
their servant for the week		9d
their drink		5d
transport of water and stone		5d
hire of one man with a horse carrying stone etc. for 1 day		3½d
hire of five men at the quarry to whom for the week 9d	3s	9d
one man for the week		8d
their drink		4d
repair of tools		4½d
bowls (*melys*) bought for drawing water at the quarry		2½d
Total	13s	10½d

Week following, *viz* next whole week before the feast
  of St Margaret [20 July]

1 quarter of sand bought		7½d
four masons working in the north quarter for the week to whom 17d	5s	8d
one mason in the same place for the week		16d
their servant for the week		9d
their drink		5d
[transport][4] of water for making mortar		3d
[one] man with one horse carrying stone etc. for 2½ days, 3½d a day		8½d
[five] men at the quarry to whom 9d for the week	3s	9d
[. . .] in the same place for the week		8d
their drink for the week		4d
making a wedge from new		5d
Total	14s	11d

[Week] following in which were the feasts of Blessed
  Mary Magdalene [22 July] and St James [25
  July], working about paving at the square
  (*pavagr' ad quadrium*)

12 seams of sand for paving at the square		3d
four masons for the week because of the said feasts 14½d	4s	10d
one mason in the same place for the week		14d
their servant for the week		7½d
their drink		4d

[4]There is a piece torn out of the left hand side of the membrane at this point.

two men carrying stone at the square with two horses for two days, 3½d a day		14d
one man with one horse carrying likewise for ½ a day		1¾d
five men at the quarry for the week because of the said feasts to whom 7½d	3s	1½d
one man in the same place for the week		7d
their drink for the week		4d
Total	12s	6¾d

Week following in which was the feast of St Peter ad Vincula [1 August]

50 seams of sand at the paving		15d
four masons working about the said paving to whom 17d for the week	5s	8d
one mason in the same place for the week		16d
their servant for the week		9d
hire of one man with one horse carrying stone at the square for 4½ days, 3½d a day		15¾d
the masons' drink for the week		5d
five men at the quarry for the week to whom 9d	3s	9d
one man in the same place for the week		8d
their drink for the week		4d
Total	15s	5¾d

Week next following in which was the feast of St Laurence [10 August]

three masons at the wall around the barbican to whom 17d for the week	4s	3d
one mason in the same place for the week		16d
their servant for the week		9d
their drink for the week		5d
carriage of stone at the wall as in the next week, *viz*		15¾d
four men at the quarry to whom 9d for the week	3s	
one man in the same place for the week		8d
their drink		4d
mending various tools		3d
transport of water for 4 days		4d
mending the conduit, *viz* firewood, pitch, tallow, and rope for the same		3d
2 lb of tin for the same		3d
one stone of lead for the same		5d
wages of the plumber at piece-work for his labour		10d
Total	14s	4¾d

[*Dorse*]
Week in which was the feast of the Assumption of
St Mary [15 August]

100 seams of sand	2s	6d
three masons at the wall to whom 17d for the week	4s	3d
one mason in the same place for the week		16d
their servant for the week		9d
their drink for the week		5d
transport of water		2d
five men at the quarry to whom 9d for the week	3s	9d
one man for the week in the same place		8d
their drink		4d
one man with one horse carrying stone at the wall for 5½ days, 3½d a day		18½d
Total	15s	8½d

Week next following in which was the feast of
St Bartholomew [24 August]

as many masons and workmen at the quarry and transport of water and carriage as in the same week next preceding		. . .
one barrow bought besides		1d
mending one vat (*vat'*)		3d
Total	16s	0½d

Week next following in which was the feast of the
Beheading of St John the Baptist [29 August]

as many masons and all other workmen still as in the same week, price of carriage nothing, and besides those things *viz*		
21 lb of Spanish iron bought for strengthening the windows in the chapel above the East Gate, price ½d a lb		10½d
wages of W. Crockern' for making frames (*virgis*) there and latches and catches (*lacch' & kacchis*)		10d
four pairs of hinges (*vertivell'*) for the said windows bought from the said W.		8d
four boards for making window shutters (*fol'*)		7d
4½ lb of lead bought for strengthening the window frames		2d
one iron wedge newly made bought with (*cum*) the said W.		4d
mending tools		2d
one large sledge bought from the said W. for the quarry	2s	2d
Sum Total	19s	11½d

Week then next following

	s	d
50 [seams of] sand		15d
11 ½ quarters of lime bought for stock, price 4d a quarter	3s	10d
three masons at the walls to whom 17d for the week	4s	3d
one mason for the week in the same place		16d
their servant for the week		9d
their drink		5d
transport of water		3d
five men at the quarry to whom 9d for the week	3s	9d
one man in the same place for the week		8d
their drink		4d
hire of one man with a horse carrying stone at the walls for the week		19d
Total	**18s**	**5d**

[Week] following in which was the feast of the Exaltation of the Holy Cross [14 September]

	s	d
[six][5] men at the quarry for the week to whom 9d	4s	6d
[one] man in the same place for the week		8d
their drink		4d
Total	**5s**	**6d**

[Week] next following in which was the feast of St Matthew [21 September]

	s	d
[. . .] as in the week next preceding, *viz* in total	5s	6d
[. . .] mending tools		5 ½d
Total	**5s**	**11 ½d**

[Week] following, *viz* the next before the feast of St Michael [29 September]

	s	d
one quarter of sand		7 ½d
two masons for the week, each 16d	2s	8d
their servant for the week		9d
their drink for the week		2 ½d
six men at the quarry to whom 9d for the week	4s	6d
two men in the same place for the week, each 8d		16d
their drink for the week		4d
Total	**10s**	**5d**

[5]There is a piece torn out of the left hand side of the membrane at this point.

Week next following

three masons at the wall for the week to whom 16d	4s	
their servant for the week		9d
their drink for the week		3d
five men at the quarry for the week to whom 9d	3s	9d
their drink for the week		3d
two men with two horses for 2 days carrying stone at the wall, each 3½d a day		14d
transport of water in that week		3d
Total	10s	5d

Week next following in which was the feast of St
  Denis [9 October]
    all and singular as in the week next preceding,
      price of carriage nothing

Total	[no amount stated]

Week next following in which was the feast of St
  Luke [18 October]

one quarter of sand		7½d
two masons for the week, each 16d	2s	8d
their servant for the week		8d
their drink for the week		2½d
five men at the quarry for the week to whom 9d	3s	9d
their drink for the week		3d
one man with one horse carrying stone at the wall for 1 day		3d
transport of water at the wall		2d
Total	8s	7d

Week next following

two masons for the week, each 16d	2s	8d
their servant for the week		8d
their drink for the week		2½d
eight men at the quarry for the week to whom 7d	4s	8d
their drink for the week		4d
Total	8s	6d

Week next following in which were the feasts of SS
  Simon and Jude the Apostles [28 October] and
  All Saints [1 November]

three masons at the walls for 2 days, 4d a day	2s	
their servant for the same time		4d
their drink for the same time		1d
six men at the quarry for the same time, 1¼d a day		15d

their drink for the same time		3d
two men with two horses carrying stone at the wall for 1 day, each 3½d a day with their drink		7d
50 [seams of] sand bought		15d
Total	5s	9d

Week following in which was the feast of St Leonard [6 November]

one quarter of sand bought		3¾d
10 quarters of lime bought, price 4d a quarter		40d
five quarters of lime bought, price 5½d a quarter	2s	3½d
three masons at the quarry to whom for the week 16d	4s	
their servant for the week		9d
their drink for the week		3¾d
transport of water		2d
four men at the quarry for the week to whom 7½d	2s	6d
one man in the same place for 1½ days		2½d
their drink for the week		5d
two men with two horses for 2½ days carrying stone at the wall, each 3¼d a day		20d
Total	15s	11½d

Week in which was the feast of St Martin [10 November], *viz* then next following

two masons for 1 day, each 2½d a day		5d
their servant for that day		1¼d
their drink for that day		0¾d
two men with two horses carrying stone at the wall for one day, each 3d a day		6d
drink of the same carriers		0½d
Total		13½d

Paid to those carrying sand for the paving by order of Thomas le Furbour then mayor in all	5s	2d
Mending the road at *Bolehill* in all, as is shown particularly in a schedule annexed hereto[6]	28s	2d
Mending the road outside the South Gate to fill it with sand, *viz* in all	7s	7d

[6]ECA Miscellaneous Roll 6 m 24

Repairing and mending the West Gate and repairing the tower next to St John's hospital and the conduit of St Peter in all, as is shown particularly in a schedule annexed hereto[7]	21s	8¾d
Seeks allowance of 4½d for parchment bought		4½d
Seeks allowance for his service this year and the year next preceding		. . .
Seeks allowance for his clerk's service		10s

Total		. . .
Total of the whole discharge		. . .

Sum total of all allowances with respect to service for two years	£28	2s	6½d
And thus there remains		76s	9½d

Schedule [1]

Expenses about the conduit outside the East Gate *viz*

four rafters bought	4d
one large beam bought 5d bought [*sic*]	2d
hire of one carpenter for 1 day	2½d
and drink	0¼d
hire of one man to assist the same carpenter for 1 day	1½d
one seam of firewood bought	2d
pitch	2d
tallow	0¾d
ropes	1d
4 lb of solder	6d
hire of one man for 2 days on account of soldering the conduit	4d
and drink	0½d
one man to assist the solderer	1d
and drink	0¼d

Expenses about the conduit in the cemetery

cor'a maior' solvit	8½d
boards for the door of the well	2d
two ties (*Tywys*) and nails for the same	2d
making the door	1d
sand to make the road for 2½ days with two horses	15d

Total	4s	3¾d

[7]ECA Miscellaneous Roll 6 m 23

Expenses of Robert Taverner *viz* about the West
    Gate

102 seams[8] loads crossed through of stone	41d
two masons for three days	18d
one man to help the said mason (*sic*) for three days	3¾d
conducting one stone to the said Gate	2d
one mason	15d
one man to help the said mason for 5½ days	6d
conducting gravel to the said gate with two horses for 1½ days	9d

About the walls

one man with one horse for one day to conduct stone to the said walls	3d
one quarter of sand	7½d
2½ quarters of lime, price 6d a quarter	15d
one servant	6d
one mason	13d
one woman [*illegible*] to transport water at the said walls	1d
Total	11s 8¼d

Cost of the tower

first week after Easter paid to workmen who worked at the tower and at the quarry[9] in that week	2s	11d
week then next following paid to two workmen who transported sand and stone to the tower for the week		10d
hire of one man[10] working in the quarry . . .[11] paid		6d
hire of one man with one horse to carry stone and sand for two days at the tower		6d
. . .[11] for one day to cast sand		1¼d
Total	4s	10d

Cost of the conduit

hire of one man in the third week following to repair (*corrigend'*) the conduit outside the East Gate, for solder and for his service	6d
one boy to serve the aforesaid man	0½d
firewood and grease bought for the same	1d

---

[8]loads crossed through
[9]*and at the quarry* written above the line
[10]illegible word written above line
[11]three illegible words omitted

Cost of the conduit
last time when the aforesaid conduit was repaired

pitch		1d
ropes for the same		0¾d
one workman to bind and make the aforesaid pipe		1d
grease for the same		0½d
Total	10s	0¾d
Sum total of this schedule	21s	8¾d

Schedule [2]
Expenses to repair the road at *Bolehille viz*

Monday next before the feast of the Exaltation
of the Holy Cross 15 horses
Tuesday following 6 horses
expenses for the aforesaid two days

bread		5½d
provisions		2½d
beer		7d
Wednesday following one horse		
expenses for that horse		1d
Thursday following ten horses		
their expenses		7½d
Friday following five horses		
and their expenses		3¾d
Monday next after the feast of the Exaltation of the Holy Cross five horses		
and their expenses		3¾d
Tuesday following four horses		
and their expenses		3d
hire of one man with his horse for four days, 3½d a day		14d
hire of two men for two days in the next week before the feast of the Exaltation of the Holy Cross to hoe gravel, with drink		7d
hire of two men to hoe gravel for five days, 1½d a day		15d
their drink for five days, ¼d a day		2½d
hire of one man to hoe gravel in the next week before the feast of St Matthew, with drink		10d
hire of one man with his horse in the said week for five days, with drink 3½d a day		18d
Monday next after the feast of St Michael eight horses, with drink	2s	2½d
Tuesday following hire of 11 horses	2s	9d
and drink		4d
Thursday following hire of ten horses	2s	6d
and drink with workmen		3d

Saturday next following hire of eight[12] horses		16d
hire of three workmen in the next week after		
the feast of St Michael for 4 days, 1¼d a day		15d
one quarter of sand bought		7½d[13]
hire of five horses Monday next after the feast		
of St Denis		15d
their drink		1¼d
Tuesday following five horses		15d
and drink		1¼d
Wednesday five horses		15d
and drink		1¼d
Thursday following six horses		18d
and drink		1½d
one workman to hoe gravel for four days,		
1½d[14] a day with drink		6d[15]
week in which was the feast of St Edward the		
King which was the last week of work at		
Bolehill		
one man for 4½ days to hoe gravel, 1½d a day		
with drink		7d
two men with two horses to carry at *Bolehill*		
for 4½ days, each 3¼d a day with drink	2s	5d
Sum total	28s	2d

III

1343–44 ACCOUNT OF ROBERT DE BRADEWORTHY, LATELY
WARDEN OF EXE BRIDGE AT EXETER, FROM
MICHAELMAS 17 EDWARD III TO THE SAME FEAST
IN THE FOLLOWING YEAR

Received from William de Kydelond for the time of		
John Russel lately warden of the said bridge	60s	
Received from William de Kydelond, farmer of		
Crykelepytte Mylle for the whole of his time	£9	
Received from John de Sutton his colleague for the		
rent pertaining to the aforesaid bridge	8s	
Received for the rent of William de Dounne	9s	6d[1]
Received from a certain glover at the end of the		
bridge for rent	3s	

[12]ten crossed through
[13]whole entry crossed through
[14]*1¼d* crossed through
[15]illegible amount crossed through
[1]*5s* crossed through

Received from the executors of the will of John de Bovy from the bequest of the aforesaid John		2s	
Received from various waggons crossing the aforesaid bridge for the same time		3s	1d
Received from William le Taverner			20d
Total of the whole charge	£13	7s	3d

Paid for four pounds of wax bought for the chapel	2s	
For one quart² of oil for the said chapel		7d
For one oak beam bought for mending the bar above the bridge		3d
For the wage of one carpenter for the same		3d
For mending one lock at the bar		1d
For carriage of sand over the bridge for one day		3d
For bread bought to distribute for the soul of Walter Gerveys	50s	
Paid to the chaplain celebrating in the chapel etc. in part payment for his service	20s	
Total of the whole discharge	73s	5d

And thus the total of the charge exceeds the total of
the discharge by £9 13s 10d. From this he allows
himself on his account for his service and his
clerk's 13s 10d because they worked together.
And thus he owes net £9.

[Rental]

Roger atte Wille		40d
Robert Hughetone	2s	
William Wyke		40d
Adam Brasyutere		40d
Richard Olyver		40d
John Gyst	7s	
Robert Brideport	20s	
Robert Noble	6s	8d
	[½ mark]	
John Swanetone		40d
William Benet		40d
John Holle		20d
John Westecote		12d
Nicholas Parcheminere		6d
William Toppelegh		6d
Richard Wythorn	2s	
Walter Cook'		6d
Total	60s	22d

²*one pottle* crossed through

IV

1389–90 ACCOUNT OF JOHN OKRYG', RECEIVER OF THE
CASH OF THE COMMUNITY OF THE AFORESAID
TOWN [OF BARNSTAPLE], FROM MICHAELMAS IN
THE 13TH YEAR OF THE REIGN OF RICHARD II TO
THE SAME FEAST IN THE 14TH YEAR (NDRO,
B1A/3972)

Arrears

Arrears for the preceding year	£4	5s	8½d
Total	£4	5s	8½d

Internal rents

Rent of the Guildhall this year without the cellar. And no more because two stalls were not handed over	16s	
Nine stalls at the Butcher's House	70s	8d
Eight butchers' stalls now handed over this year as certified	37s	4d
Total £6	4s	

External rents

Six stalls in the churchyard hired to various men on Sundays and feasts	20s	
Various stalls handed over to various men in the High Street	31s	
Fish stalls this year	18s	6d
Total	69s	6d

Sale of grazing

Meadow and grazing sold in *La Portmerssh* this year with *barbygan*	44s	3d
Grazing next to the Castle hired to Geoffrey Bythewod	10s	
Total	54s	3d

Sale of fishery

Nothing for fishery this year

Total [blank]

Profits of the court

Fines and amercements of the mayor's court this year	£7	15s
Total	£7	15s
Sum total of receipts	£24 8s	5½d

Rents paid

To the bailiff of the town for frugabul for the Butchers' House		1½d
To the keeper of Barnstaple Long Bridge for the said house	2s	
To the keeper of St Nicholas for the same house		4d
To the bailiff of the town for the fish stalls	2s	3d
To the prior of Barnstaple for the Guildhall	3s	
To John Raysshlegh for the said house	2s	
To the keeper of the Long Bridge for the Guildhall	3s	
To the prior of Barnstaple for the Butchers' House		18d
Total	14s	9½d

Expenses of the seneschal for the court of St Michael

Expenses of the seneschal in bread		18d
Ale		14d
Wine	6s	1½d
Fish	5s	9½d
Pepper and saffron [*croc'*]		5½d
Almonds		9d
Rice		5d
Sugar		2d
Sandalwood [*Sandr'*]		2d
Honey		1d
One *staynn'*		3d
Spice		2d
Raisins		2d
Garlic		0½d
Salt		1d
Firewood		4d
Stipend of John Cuacker		8d
To Robert Niel		3d
Pistr camp . . .		4½d
Ham [*Parn*]		7½d
Eggs		3d
Candles		2d
Total	18s	7d

Foreign expenses

Account for the expenses of Warin Walgrave the lord's seneschal on Passion Sunday		
Bread		21¼d
Beer		8d
Wine	8s	
Fish	4s	7d

	s	d
Almonds		12d
Rice		3d
Figs and dates		5d
Pepper and saffron		4d
Ginger		1d
Salt		2d
Firewood		2d
Expenses of the same Warin the following Tuesday		
Bread		12d
Beer		2d
Wine	4s	
Fish	2s	10d
Almonds and rice		5d
Pepper and saffron		2d
Expenses of the same Warin the Tuesday following		
Bread		5½d
Wine	2s	10d
Fish	2s	2½d
Oil		2d
Expenses of the same Warin the Thursday following		
Bread		4d
Wine		20d
Fish		7d
Pepper saffron and rice		3d
Almonds		3d
To John Bydewill and Richard Tonecote going to Exeter to the Lent assize	6s	8d
To John Bydewill, John Hunte, John Tannere and Richard Tonecote going to Exeter in the week of Pentecost before the justices of the peace of the lord king for three days	12s	
To Joice Antony and Nicholas Boghe going to Exeter to the assize of St Peter ad Vincula	12s	
To a servant of Sir James Chuddelegh by order of the mayor	6s	8d
Expenses of Nicholas . . .	4s	7d
To John Colyn	6s	8d
To Robert Hille	6s	8d
To John Copleston' for his pension	26s	. . .
For rendering account in the lord king's exchequer for the mayor	4s	8d
To the hundred bailiffs on two occasions by order of the mayor	4s	
For one common sack [*sacco*]		6d
For one key for the chamber of the clerk of the place		2d
To Adam Smith for repair of one bushel		8d
To Adam Bacoun for writing one copy		8d
To Thomas Lane by order of the mayor	6s	8d

		£	s	d
Total		£6	16s	8d

Custom[of] 'le Clok'

For unpressed [*mer'*] wine bought		13s	2d
Tables bought		4s	1d
Iron bought		14s	8½d
Carbuncle bought		7s	2½d
Various colours		8s	2½d
To Richard Thomelyn, William Feraunt, Adam Mole and Henry Bratton on various occasions to break and repair the walls of the belfry		3s	2d
Two cords bought		2s	2d
Silk			1½d
35 lb of *ence* thus 2½d per lb		7s	3½d
Tin bought	£3		9d
Lead bought		10s	
One lock bought			9d
To Adam Raw		104s	
loc' P Total	£9	2s	1½d

Custom of the pillory

For unpressed wine bought		30s	2d
To John Pope and other carpenters hired about the pillory at assessment		33s	4d
For wine paid to the bailiff of Sherwill [*Shyrewill*]			8d
Other services			4d
To John Hurd for carriage of unpressed wine from *Chyddecomb* to Barnstaple [*Barum*]		6s	8d
The same place for putting the said unpressed wine in quarts			7½d
Carrying the same wine to the churchyard			15½d
Tables bought		3s	8d
200 hatch nails [*haychnayll'*]			6½d
To John Wodelond for colouring the pillory			6d
Rushes, tallow and ochre with one pot [*olla*] and firewood		3s	8d
Two quarts of *tallet*		2s	8d
Stone tiles		3s	7d
A latch and three keys		3s	3d
Sand			2d
[. . .]			12d
John Cornyssh to cover the pillory at assessment		2s	3d
For *oneselath*			5d
Total	£4	14s	9½d

Custom of the Butchers' House and fish stalls

For repair of the Butchers' House and fish stalls	12d
And for the plastering [*p'gac'*] of the said house	2d
Total	14d

Officers' wages

To the mayor for his pension this year	40s	
To the receiver and the mayor's clerk	13s	4d
For making the account	6s	8d
For parchment for indentures between the mayor and the receiver and for the receiver's account and for writing one copy	[figure not given]	

Total		60s	7½d
Total of all expenses and [lib?]	£26	8s	1¼d

And thus it exceeds by 39s 7¾ d. And afterwards allowed to the same 6d which cannot be levied and 3s 4d for grazing and thus it exceeds by 43s 5¾d.

PAGE REFERENCES TO SECTIONS

	1304–6	1339–40	1341–2	1342–3	1344–5	1347–8	1348–9	1349–50	1350–1	1351–2	1352–3
Income											
Arrears	1	4	—	19	25	32	40	—	—	—	—
Fixed rents	1,3	4	12	19	25	33	40	46	54	67	76
Issues (Customs)	1,3	4	12	20	26	33	40	47	54	68	76
Profits of the courts	1,3	4	13	20	26	33	40	47	55	68	76
Foreign receipts	1	5	—	—	—	—	—	—	—	—	—
Expenditure											
Rents paid	2	5	14	21	31	33	41	48	55	69	78
Rent deficits/ rents allowed	2	6	13	20	26	—	44	51	59	68	77
Necessary expenses	2	7	15	21	27	34	42	49	56	71	80
Fees	2	11	18	24	31	36	41	48	55	69	78
Serjeants' allowances	—	6	14	21	31	—	—	52	60	73	81
Gifts and presents	3	10	17	23	29	36	—	48	57	71	79
(Foreign) expenses and payments	3	8	16	22	28	—	42	50	57, 58	70	79
Expenses of the chapel above the East Gate	—	—	—	—	—	—	—	—	—	—	79
Expenses about the walls	—	—	—	—	—	—	—	—	—	72	—

GENERAL INDEX

References are to page numbers in the introduction (roman numerals) and in the text (arabic numerals). A page reference may imply more than one reference to the page in question. Places, except for well-known cities, are in Devon unless the county is specified. Subjects not found in their alphabetical place in this index may be sought under one of the following chief subject headings:

Building materials
Exeter
Fees paid
Food and drink
Gifts

AFFETON (Aftone), 30; Hugh de, 49, 71
Albe Marlea (Aumarle), William de, 49, 82
Ale, selling of *see* Customs recipts: brithgavel
Alum, bales of, xxvii, 44
Ambrose, Sir, 16; *and see* Nyweburgh, Sir Ambrose of
Amercements, x, xiv, xvii, 3, 5–7, 13–14, 20–21, 33, 40, 45, 50, 52–53, 57, 60–61, 64, 68, 72–77, 79, 81, 85, 112; *and see* Bakers, amercements of
Antony, Joice, 114
'Apprentices' of the law *see* Barristers
Arblaster, Richard le, 28
Archdeacons/archdeaconries *see* Cornwall; Exeter; Totnes; Wells
Archers, for the king's service, 29, 37
Arrears received and paid, x, xxiv, 1, 4–5, 9, 19, 25, 31–32, 40, 83–84, 87, 112
Arundel, earl of, xxiii, 30
Atte Forde *see* Forde
Atte Wille *see* Wille
Atte Wode *see* Wode
Assizes, xxi, xxvii, 9–11, 18, 22–24, 29–30, 35, 37–38, 43, 48–49, 57–58, 71, 87–88
Audelegh, Sir James de, 23
Auditors of the accounts, xxix, 19, 25, 32, 39, 46, 54
Aumarle *see* Albe Marlea
Auncel, William, sheriff of Devon, 79
Ayleward, Alfred, 19
Aysch (Aysche, Ayssch), (Sir) Alan de, 37, 39; John, 74

BAA, Henry de, 36
Bacoun, Adam, 114
Bagavel *see* Customs receipts: bagavel
Bakere, Ralph, 66; Thomas, 66; Walter, 67
Bakers, amercements of, xiv, 5, 33, 40, 45, 47, 55, 66, 68, 74, 77, 84
Ballok', John, 72–73

Barbour, Henry, 66; Matthew, 62–63
Barnstaple, customs of, 115; prior of, 113; receiver of *see* Okryg', John; receiver's account, 112–116; St Michael's court expenses, 113–114; St Nicholas, keeper of, 113; streets and buildings, 112–113, 115
Barristers ('apprentices' of the law), xxvii
Batteshull (Battishulle), Martin, xx, 50, 58 *and see* Martin, the clerk
Bavy, William, 52
Bayg', Walter, 65
Beaminster (Bemynstr', Bymynstr', Bymystr', Bymystre), Robert (de), xi, 24, 32, 41, 57 *and see* Brideport, Robert de (sometimes known as Robert de Beaminster)
Beauson, Beatrice, 28
Bedman, Adam, 61
Bedyngton, Sir Ralph de, 36
Bek', Robert (de), 38
Bemynstr' *see* Beaminster
Benet, William, 46 and note, 75, 111
Beridon(e), John (de), 40, 74–75
Berlegh, Ralph, 65
Bersham, Philip de, xxviii, 22
Berwyk', Hugh de, 29
Beyvyn, xxi; John, 65; Richard, 65; Roger, 93; Stephen, 1, 3
Bikelegh (Bykelegh, Bykeleygh), William (de), 2, 6, 13, 20–21, 26, 59, 68, 77, 85, 91
[Bishop's] Clyst *see* Clyst [Bishop's]
Black Death (plague), xi–xiii, xv, xix note, xxi–xxii, xxvii
Blaunchecote, Robert, 90
Boghe, Nicholas, 114
Bollegh (Bollek'), (Sir) Henry de, archdeacon of Cornwall, 2, 6, 13, 20, 26, 85, 91
Bollok', Stephen, 62, 67, 81
Bolset, Thomas, 51

119